Rites of Life

The Scientific Evidence for Life Before Birth

Other Books by David Rorvik
The Good Housekeeping Woman's Medical Guide

Other Books by Landrum B. Shettles and David Rorvik
Choose Your Baby's Sex
Your Baby's Sex: Now You Can Choose

Rites of Life

The Scientific Evidence for
Life Before Birth

Landrum B. Shettles, M.D., Ph.D.
With
David Rorvik

Zondervan Publishing House
a Division of The Zondervan Corporation
Grand Rapids, Michigan

RITES OF LIFE
Copyright © 1983 by Landrum B. Shettles and David Rorvik
Published by The Zondervan Corporation
Grand Rapids, Michigan

Library of Congress Cataloging in Publication Data
Shettles, Landrum B. (Landrum Brewer), 1909–
     Rites of life.

     Bibliography: p.
     Includes index.
     1. Pregnancy—Moral and ethical aspects.   2. Abortion—
Moral and ethical aspects.   I. Rorvik, David M.
II. Title.   [DNLM: 1. Abortion, Induced.   2. Embryo.
3. Fetus.   4. Philosophy, Medical. WQ 210 S554r]
RG556.S48   1983   363.4'6   83-19716
ISBN 0-310-27990-9

Edited by James E. Ruark
Designed by Ann Cherryman and James E. Ruark

83 84 85 86 87 88 / 9 8 7 6 5 4 3 2 1

Printed in the United States of America

Leo Tolstoy believed that art's highest purpose is to make men good—by choice. It is to the spirit of that belief that we dedicate this book, and to the greatest art of all: unfolding human life.

Contents

Introduction
A Celebration of Life in the Midst of Debate

By David Rorvik

This book is about human life—from conception to birth. It is intended to be a guide, to instruct the reader on the biological requisites of human life, the fascinating complexities of its emergence, and the purposeful progress of its development in the womb. In both words and pictures, this book is a celebration of that life, an expression of awe in the presence of so much purpose and meaning, an exclamation of joy in the attendance of an unfolding biological reality so complex, yet resolute, that it seems almost to be imbued with magic or invested with miracles. The book is written in the frank hope that readers everywhere will come, if only by degrees, to know life better and thus love it more.

Inevitably, the book cannot help but be concerned with the debate that now rages with respect to abortion. Superficially at least, that debate centers on the question of *when* life begins. In reality, as Dr. Shettles will show, it is about something more than that; it is about the value society *chooses* to place on human life at various stages and under various cir-

9

cumstances. It is about a shift in private and public morality. It is about a potentially epochal, though still incomplete, displacement of one world view by another. Some perceive of this shift in broad terms of sociological law gradually replacing natural law; others perceive of it in the perhaps sharper focus of a "quality-of-life" ethic threatening to prevail over a "sanctity-of-life" ethic.

Much of the abortion debate, Dr. Shettles believes, is beside the point—which is life itself. It is his primary objective in this book to put life's story on these pages and let it speak for itself. He is convinced that knowledge and understanding of the intrinsic order and beauty of life, from its earliest incandescence at the time of conception onward, will do more to constructively shape opinion than any court or legislation can ever hope to do.

I feel genuinely privileged to have been associated with Dr. Shettles, as both a friend and a co-author, for the past fifteen years. During that time I have been deeply impressed by the scope of his scientific work and moved by his uncompromising personal integrity. If anyone had suggested ten years ago that the day would come when I would work with Dr. Shettles on a book that would reach conclusions that are anti-abortion, my reaction would have been scornful at best. But Dr. Shettles, I have discovered, is a man who has surprising effects on people. Perhaps this is because he is so surprising himself. Consider these excerpts from two publications and you will begin to understand the man:

"The birth of the world's first 'test-tube' baby—Louise Brown—last summer wouldn't have been such a shocker," *Science News* reported in 1980,

> if more people had realized that human *in vitro* [literally, "in glass," meaning test tube or other laboratory container] fertilization research efforts had already been underway for a number of years. . . . Actually, the idea of human *in vitro* fertilization, Melvin L. Taymor of Harvard Medical School explains, had its inception in 1955 with Landrum B. Shettles.[1]

[1]Vol. 115 (1980):358.

Saturday Review observed:

> The issues about test-tube babies are not new. . . . This event [the birth of Louise Brown] was ironically juxtaposed in the news with a lawsuit in New York brought by the couple who might themselves have become the parents of the world's first test-tube baby six years earlier. In 1972, Dr. Landrum Shettles, of the Columbia-Presbyterian Medical Center in New York, removed an egg from a Florida woman, Doris Del Zio, and fertilized it *in vitro* with her husband's sperm. . . . But Shettles' experiment was aborted—in both the meanings— when his superior, Dr. Raymond Vande Wiele, destroyed it. Perhaps Vande Wiele was indignant that Shettles was "playing God" in this fashion; but in the view of the Del Zios, it was Vande Wiele himself who was playing God by destroying their potential baby. Surprisingly, Mrs. Del Zio was awarded $50,000 . . . which suggests that the jurors were at least convinced that the "test tube" attempt was neither preposterous nor immoral.[2]

These news accounts point up two facts: (1) Dr. Shettles was one of the first persons to directly study, close up and first-hand, the biological events that attend the creation of human life; and (2) he has been involved in research which raises certain bioethical issues not unrelated to abortion. Dr. Shettles began his studies of human conception and early development in the 1940s. By 1954, at which time he had already reported upon the successful fertilization of a human egg by a human sperm in the test tube, he attended the International Fertility Conference in Italy. The Pope took that occasion to pointedly condemn those who "take the Lord's work" into their "own hands." Even such liberals as novelist-gadfly Norman Mailer wondered, many years later, in the 1970s, whether people like Shettles (whom he singled out by name) weren't "fixing to operate on the Lord."

Ironically, it was the very studies that some condemned and others feared that ultimately convinced Dr. Shettles of the meaningfulness of life before birth and consolidated his opposition to abortion. The early test-tube fertilization work,

[2](October 28, 1978):10.   **11**

he explains, was not motivated by a desire "to play God," but rather, to understand the dynamics of human conception and embryology from the standpoint, first, of gaining basic knowledge and, second, of treating various forms of infertility. His micrographs of life's beginnings now appear in more than fifty medical texts worldwide and hang, in greatly enlarged form, in the American Museum of Natural History in New York, in the Museum of Science in Boston, and in the Academy of Sciences in Moscow.

Contributions to Science

Dr. Shettles' contributions to human embryology and reproductive science have been widely acknowledged. Dr. John Rock, one of the principal developers of the birth-control pill, said of Dr. Shettles' test-tube work: "He is the only man in the world who could show you what he has shown you and tell you what he has told you of the very first stages of human conception. His *in vitro* fertilization of oocytes [eggs] and culture of resulting embryos is a landmark in our insight into human embryogenesis."

Dr. S. B. Gusberg stated, while professor and chairman of the Department of Obstetrics and Gynecology at the Mount Sinai School of Medicine in New York: "I have known Dr. Landrum Shettles and his scientific work for many years, and I consider him to be an extraordinarily able investigator in the morphology of reproductive biologic phenomena . . . whose work through the years has enabled the documentation of a number of morphologic phenomena related to fertilization and implantation."

The late Dr. Alan G. Guttmacher, a world leader in the field of obstetrics and gynecology and one of the principal forces behind Planned-Parenthood–World Population, said: "Dr. Shettles has an ingenious mind and superb technical ability. . . . My relations with him have been warm and rewarding."

Science writer Robert Weil, reviewing Dr. Shettles' career, described him as "one of the twentieth century's titans in the field of female infertility." And Albert Rosenfeld, author and former science editor of *Life* magazine, has called Dr. Shettles "a genius ahead of his time" (*Omni, December 1982*).

Dr. Shettles says of his own work: "I feel privileged to have had a front-row seat at the spectacle of life." He was one of the first to investigate the morphology (form and structure) of the human sex cells: egg and sperm. For decades he studied and published on their physiology and their metabolic requirements under various circumstances and in various environments. Concurrently he studied the dynamics of egg and sperm interaction in the fertilization process. He was the first to achieve *in vitro* fertilization of human eggs consistently. His studies shed important light on a number of previously hidden aspects of human fertility and infertility. His studies helped establish what constitutes normal sperm count and behavior. They also revealed a good deal about the biomechanisms of implantation, those events that are required for the newly fertilized egg to attach itself to the lining of the womb. His detailed studies of pregnancy at every stage provided information on a variety of complications that can attend pregnancy—information necessary to prevent such complications. His exploration of the development of the zygote, embryo, and fetus from conception to birth, day-by-day, provided the world with what he has called one of its first "biological atlases."

Well before the Supreme Court made its ruling on abortion in 1973, Dr. Shettles' studies of life's beginnings had imposed upon him, in his words, "the burdens and joys of knowledge." This, he relates, was a knowledge of life-before-birth that made it impossible for him to sanction abortion. But until New York State passed a liberalizing abortion law in 1970, there was little reason to speak out against abortion. Most states still prohibited it or made it available only in extreme circumstances. When New York became what some called "the abortion capital of the world" in 1970, Dr. Shettles, then practicing in New York, did not perform any abortions himself and urged patients who requested them to reconsider. He argued that the baby could be given up for adoption after birth, as there were, as his own practice demonstrated, many childless couples who desperately wanted babies.

It wasn't until 1973 that Dr. Shettles felt compelled to make a public statement in opposition to abortion. He criticized the Supreme Court decision in a letter that was published in the *New York Times*. He considered the ruling scientifically misinformed and said so, concluding his letter: "To deny a truth should not be made a basis for legalizing abortion." The ruling offended not only Dr. Shettles' sense of morality, but his scientific sensibility as well. He took exception in particular to the Court's declaration that it was not possible to determine when human life begins. When a former colleague—a man who had risen to a position of some prominence in the federal government—called him to suggest that "you owe the justices an apology" for the *Times* letter, Dr. Shettles firmly declined to retract his criticism.

Some might question Dr. Shettles' position in light of his "test-tube" baby research. After all, doesn't the creation of embryos in the laboratory pose ethical problems? What happens to the embryos at the end of the research? Isn't their destruction the same as abortion? These were questions that Dr. Shettles began asking himself in the wake of the 1973 Court ruling. That ruling and his own opposition to it made him think hard about his own research.

In the early days of Dr. Shettles' research—in the fifties and sixties—the need for the *in vitro* work had seemed clear enough. Medical students were still studying human conception and embryogenesis indirectly—by looking at pictures of various animal embryos and fetuses, for example. Dr. Shettles' work changed all of that, making direct study possible for the first time. Gradually, however, the more Dr. Shettles learned about what it was that he was doing and observing, the more he began privately questioning the morality of jettisoning what many scientists call "bench embryos"—those created in the laboratory and then discarded at the end of an experiment or project. It was deeply rewarding to watch human life begin and unfold under the microscope, something else again when that life—a human embryo—was unable to be sustained any longer outside the womb and thus was discarded along with the laboratory culture in which it had revealed some of its secrets as it grew. Commenting on that dilemma, Dr. Shettles quotes a line from an essay by Alexander Pope: "It was 'like following life through creatures you dissect: you lose it in the moment you detect.' "[3]

Dr. Settles' soul-searching finally forced him to conclude that no human life should be created in the laboratory unless there is the definite intention of implanting it in a human womb for the purpose of trying to overcome otherwise intractable infertility. The efforts might fail, he concedes, "but then, so do many of Mother Nature's." He states that he cannot believe there is anything immoral about trying to create life where there is "the desire for it and the opportunity for it."

In recent years Dr. Shettles has sought alternatives to test-tube conceptions for the treatment of various forms of infertility. In fact, he has recently devised a procedure by which many of the same women who are candidates for "test-tube" babies can become pregnant without the risks inherent in the test-tube conception and laboratory culturing of embryos. At the same time, he is actively pursuing the possibility of embryo *transplants* which also avoid the dangers of *in vitro* fertilization. The idea is to transplant embryos directly from women who don't want them to women who do, thus not only salvaging lives that would be wasted via abortion, but also giving otherwise infertile women an opportunity to bear children through a unique program of "prenatal adoption."

A Change of Viewpoint

As for my own position on abortion, I recall feeling strongly about it as early as 1965—strongly in *favor* of it. As the editor of a college daily newspaper that year, I enraged many normally peaceful people by publishing an editorial column under the heading, "Abort, Girls, Abort!" Later on, after graduate

[3]*Moral Essays,* Ep. I, 29.

school and a stint as a science and medical reporter at *Time* magazine, I traveled to Uganda on an assignment from *Look* magazine to investigate some new drugs that were being developed there. These were the "prostaglandins," a biochemical family of substances that many people—myself included—hoped would finally provide the ideal means of inducing abortion. (Since then, they have, in fact, come into use for that purpose.) Upon returning to the United States and publishing my report, I was invited to appear on the "Dick Cavett Show" to argue, in league with Germaine Greer, author of *The Female Eunuch,* the merits of legal abortion. I readily agreed to do so and enjoyed throwing myself into the debate.

Later, in other articles, I helped spread the message that unless we did something soon we were going to "breed ourselves into extinction." It had been my view for some time that overpopulation was the root of most, if not all, evils. Abortion, of course, was one of the primary "solutions" I proposed.

I was not entirely unhappy when a religious figure labeled me a "secular humanist" and a "biological reductionist." I wasn't entirely sure what those terms implied, but they seemed to suggest that I was looking to man, not God, for answers to human problems and that I had reduced man to mere biological matter in my philosophical scheme of things— biological matter that could be manipulated at will, by man himself, and remade in any image that suited society's desires at any given time. If that *was* what was being ascribed to me, it was not far off the mark.

For years I was an eager proponent of the utilitarian ethic, particularly in matters biological and—even more specifically—reproductive. I was always guided in my pro-abortion zeal by a desire to secure what I felt was best for society. I had genuine difficulty fathoming the sort of mind that was— as I imagined—so rigid and inhumane that it would place over the lives, liberties, and happiness of suffering womankind something as immaterial and ghostly as mere "potential human life." Regrettably, I was not at all reluctant to try to tar those who were opposed to abortion as "religious fanatics." More than once I voiced the opinion—still heard in some quarters today—that abortion is essentially "a Catholic issue," that the Church is more interested in adding new members to its rolls than it is in improving the quality of the lives of its followers.

Abortion appeared to me—and still does to many people—to be a highly economic solution to a number of vexatious social problems. But I had other reasons for supporting abortion. As one who regarded himself as an "enlightened liberal male," I had long since hoisted the banner of the "sexual revolution." I had accounted the Pill no less significant in its own round little way than the Wheel had been some centuries earlier. Suddenly it was possible, with a convenience unprecedented in history, to separate "recreational" sex from the procreational variety. It seemed logical to make abortion another fixture of the "revolution," a backup measure when the Pill failed or a careless revolutionary forgot to take it.

In all of this there was an element of male guilt and self-interest it took me some years to sort out. When I declared that a woman had "a right to her own body" when it came to abortion, I was conveniently excusing the considerable role the male might play in a pregnant woman's predicament. When I proclaimed that the abortion decision should be a woman's alone, I neatly exchanged for "gallantry" whatever guilt I might dimly have perceived. As Robert Louis Stevenson said, "The devil, depend upon it, can sometimes do a very gentlemanly thing." Looking back, I'm rather certain that more than a few unexpectedly pregnant women, abruptly confronted by the "gallant" absence of the male during the abortion, must have harbored some secret doubts concerning the new chivalry.

My writing in the late sixties and early seventies was characterized by an abiding faith in the ability of technology to solve most of society's problems. I wrote optimistically of "morning-after" and "month-after" birth-control pills; of scenarios hatched by "think tanks" and government committees that would make birth control mandatory by putting chemicals in the water and supplying the antidote on a selective basis; of a Nobel Prize winner's program of "germinal choice," which amounted to a plan whereby only the "most fit" would breed and lesser mortals would dutifully abstain in the interests of "the greater good"; of the capability of "genetic engineering" to remake man someday in whatever image he chose for himself; of psychosurgery and "electronic stimulation of the brain" to "correct" and even prevent criminal behavior. If man could not be "good"—and behave "rationally"—on his own, then technology could *make* him good and be "cost-effective" in the bargain. If the "ends" were "the greatest good for the greatest number," then the "means" were justified, whatever they might be.

I was a long time losing my love of situation ethics. Had my livelihood not depended upon my constant surveillance of the technologies I wrote about, I might never have seen or heard enough to convince me that the "solutions" beloved by so many "liberal" technocrats were susceptible, not only to spectacular failure, but to awesome abuse. It gradually became clear to me that shortcuts which were supposed to be saving society time and money were going to cost people their freedoms. Only the short-sighted could be comforted by the fact that those thus deprived would *at first* be those made largely invisible to conscience by virtue of some mental or physical state of "incompetence," by criminality or "potential criminality," or by poverty so extreme there was no lobby for it.

In a series of articles I admitted, in effect, that I had been wrong about a great many things. Those articles reflected my reexamination of an ethic that was mindless of *individual* freedom and ultimately destructive to a society founded on the concept of that freedom. No longer did I believe that by zapping the nonconforming brain with a few "corrective kilovolts" could men be made "good." Instead I wrote of self-described "liberal" Ivy League researchers collaborating with Nixon bureaucrats and CIA technicians in pursuit of scenarios that would invade the privacy of the mind and rob it of its essence—all in the name, of course, of preventing crime. I decried various other "solutions" I had previously embraced.

The ideas put forward by a number of Nobel Prize winners for "planned eugenics" began to strike me as not only naive but patently dangerous, even catastrophic: active efforts

18

to "improve" the human race through selective/restrictive breeding; through the elimination of "defectives" via abortion, infanticide, and euthanasia ("mercy killing"); and ultimately through direct genetic manipulation. Nobelists James Watson and Francis Crick, co-discoverers of the structure of DNA, the "basic stuff of life," have at different times proposed leaving open the option of killing newborn infants if they are badly defective or fail to pass various genetic tests. Linus Pauling, twice a Nobel Prize winner, has suggested that carriers of certain genetic defects should have symbols of those defects tattooed on their foreheads so that they could be restrained, either by their own volition or through legislation, from marrying and reproducing.

The "quality" of life that the social engineers offered us, it seemed to me, was being purchased at the expense of what makes life itself worth having: diversity, creativity, liberty. One day I dug out an article I had been saving; I'd kept it because I had thought of writing a rebuttal that would have defended some of the eugenicists named in it. The article, "The Specter of Eugenics," was written by Charles Frankel, then Old Dominion professor of philosophy and public affairs at Columbia University. Though there were still a few points with which I would quibble, I now found myself in complete agreement with Frankel's eloquent conclusion:

> The partisans of large-scale eugenic planning, the Nazis aside, have usually been people of notable humanitarian sentiments. They seem not to hear themselves. It is that other music that they hear, the music that says that there shall be nothing random in the world, nothing independent, nothing moved by its own vitality, nothing out of keeping with some Idea; even our children must be not our progeny but our creations.[4]

The concept of "the perfect man," "the perfect child," the liberal/technological dream no longer loomed lustrous on my horizon. Indeed, I began increasingly to value imperfection, the unexpected, the random, the diverse. In a controversial

[4]*Commentary* (March 1974):33.

book published in 1978, I reported that a human being had been cloned (reproduced through the stimulation of a single body-cell nucleus rather than via the union of two sex cells). I readily admitted that this was my *belief,* based on interviews with some of the people involved in the clandestine project and on some observation of their research, and that I could not prove that it had happened. I stated in the book that I expected the story to be doubted but hoped that it would stimulate a public debate on the entire field of genetic engineering. The book (*In his Image,* Lippincott) did spark an extended international debate, causing me to further refine my ideas about a number of bioethical issues that I had acknowledged with a certain ambivalence in the book.

In an article I wrote sometime later called "Predestinations" (*Omni,* October 1980), I said there were genuine dangers in the new genetic work, but not of the sort that were commonly being discussed. Test-tube babies were not going to force a dehumanizing redefinition of mankind; human clones were never going to overrun the earth. And for the time being at least, the gene tinkerers were in little danger of accidentally creating some recombinant microhorror that would peril the earth with exotic new disease.

The real danger, I believed, was the temptation to use the new technology to *level* the human experience, to "weed out" certain "unproductive" or "obsolete" human types, to create a monotonous monoculture of "perfect" human specimens. In a society increasingly short on imagination and compassion, diversity seemed to be rapidly becoming confused with *adversity.*

The marriage of technology to situation ethics was, I wrote, promising us "solutions" that were advertised as "cost-effective," but which were more likely only cosmetic. Instead of dealing with the root causes of violence—poverty, lack of education, etc.—we try for the cheap way out, short-circuiting brains with drugs and psychosurgery, which are merely new variations of a failed theme: restraint. Instead of improving our diets and cleaning up our environment as means of eradicating cancer at its origins, we look for a chemical "magic bullet" that will control the disease and permit us to go on polluting ourselves and our world. Eventually we should be able to redesign ourselves, through genetic tinkering, in such a way that we can *tolerate* almost all of the undesirable "side effects" of what we call "progress." I wrote woefully of a recombinant microorganism someone had already dreamed up that would make garbage smell good, as "cost-effective" (and as illusory) a solution to one of the problems of urban decay as any social planner could imagine.

I concluded that the new technologies would not make man more noble, more compassionate, more aware of his own diverse mystery, but rather, more tolerant of social and environmental rot. If there was a "super race" on the way it would not be the product of a mad dictator's dream, but the cost-analyzed, market-tested, supposedly pragmatic product of the scientist-social planner. Blue eyes and blond hair would not be a fraction as important as the ability to endure stenches, stress, bad food, crowding, industrial pollution, boredom, and depersonalization.

The "New Man," in my view, would be remarkably stable, nonviolent (except in "humane" ways, of course, and then only in the interests of "quality of life"), defect-free and—like the New Bread that is already with us—bland, short on real content, processed, refined, whitened, artificially preserved, and baked to absolute uniformity of texture. And— the greatest tragedy of all—no one could doubt him when he claimed to be perfectly happy.

It seems to me that the seeds are already being planted. If they are permitted to grow, these seeds will give rise to a world in which consciousnesss, in a very real sense, will cease to be singular and "life" will assume a homogeneous unity that will reduce man, stripped of the individuality by which he defines and knows and changes himself, to a sterile, static biomass scarcely aware of its own existence. The "solutions" that I have abandoned are those which seem always to *limit* man's experience, *dim* his consciousness, and by removing challenge, *reduce* his chance of becoming something greater than he can ever imagine.

Even if all of this had not been enough to induce me to gradually reevaluate my position on abortion—as a consequentialist given, perhaps by a quirk of nature or a survivalist's gene, to taking the *long* view—I hope I might eventually have recognized that in a society that starts out killing life-in-the-womb and then—"humanely"—begins creeping up on infanticide and "mercy killing," nobody, including myself, might be safe. Beyond that, I had the "misfortune"—in large part because of my association with Dr. Shettles—to know more than average of what was going on in the pregnant womb. With my vision no longer filtered through an ethic that had comfortably distorted "the picture," sometimes even rendering it invisible, I was finally forced to see and deal with what had been there all along: human life.

Part 1

Life Itself

The world will never starve for want of wonders, but only for want of wonder.

—G. K. Chesterton

Not all of us will live to be old, but we were each once a fetus. We had some engaging qualities which unfortunately we lost as we grew older. We were supple and physically active. We were not prone to disc lesions and were not obese. Our most depraved vice was thumbsucking, and . . . we ruled our mothers with a serene efficiency which our fathers could not hope to emulate. Our main handicap in a world of adults was that we were small, naked, nameless and voiceless. But surely if any of us count for anything now, we counted for something before we were born.

—Dr. Albert W. Liley,
"Father of Fetology"

1

Is There Life Before Conception?

A Look at the Sexiest Cells in the Body

Getting the Picture

The woman was still talking to the doctor when he ushered her into the hall. She was looking for some further reassurance, and the doctor was giving it to her. Her worry lines relaxed a little as he spoke.

"At seven weeks," he was saying, "it's just a tiny mass of cells; you wouldn't even recognize it; there's nothing human about it at that stage."

I didn't have to guess what the conversation was about.

Some weeks later, while preparing a paper for publication, I asked my colleague—the same person who had spoken to the woman in the hall—to examine a photograph I intended to include in my paper. It was a picture of a human fetus. I asked the doctor, an internist, to guess how old the fetus was. I couldn't tell whether the startled look on his face had more to do with the picture or the question.

Nonetheless, he squinted at the color slide and said, "About twelve or thirteen weeks."

"No," I responded. "Closer to seven weeks."   **25**

The doctor looked even more startled, but didn't say anything, though he did study the slide for several more moments. Later he admitted he was taken aback by "how human" even a seven-week-old fetus looks. He added that he had not "paid much attention" to fetal details in the past and asked to see other slides of embryos and fetuses. It was evident that as he studied those slides he was examining as well some of his own inner images, his preconceptions about human life.

"Getting the picture," as I term it, can have profound effects on people. There are a lot of clichés to partially describe these effects: "A picture is worth a thousand words," "Seeing is believing," etc. What it all comes down to is full and free access to evidence, a concept that has long been held sacred in our courts. Yet, when it comes to making important decisions about human life in the womb, we are often told that the most important evidence of all should be withheld.

All of this, including my encounter with the young internist some years ago, was brought home to me afresh when an article appeared recently in the *New England Journal of Medicine*.[1] What the article said was this: When women are shown ultrasound images of their unborn babies, they very often experience what has been called the "shock of recognition," recognition that what they are seeing is human life and that it belongs to them. They identify or "bond" with the unborn baby after seeing even a fuzzy picture of it in the womb. The article noted that once this visual bond occurs, women who had planned to have abortions are likely to reconsider. Even women who knew they were at considerable risk of giving birth to defective children expressed a desire to have their babies, rather than have abortions, after viewing the ultrasound images.

Remarkably, however, one of the authors of this article, Dr. Mark I. Evans, told the *Los Angeles Times* that in his own medical practice, he would not show the ultrasound pictures

[1]J. P. Fletcher and M. I. Evans, "Maternal Bonding in Early Fetal Ultrasound Examinations," in *New England Journal of Medicine*, vol. 308:392-393.

of their fetuses to women who intend to have abortions. "I don't want to bias them unfairly," he was quoted. "I believe women should have an abortion if that is their choice." But surely, what is truly unfair, both to the woman and to the fetus, is to *withhold* evidence. If a woman is to be given the opportunity to make a truly informed choice, she should be apprised of precisely what it is that she plans to abort. The *real* "unfair bias" occurs when a woman is denied full access to the facts.

I have seen, time and again, in my own practice the beneficial effects "full disclosure" can have on both mother and child. And on the father too, for that matter. I have always encouraged expectant mothers and fathers to learn as much as they can about the life they are nurturing in the womb—both through pictures of fetal development at each stage, and through factual accounts of what is transpiring along the way. The more these prospective parents learn, the more excited they invariably become. I firmly believe these individuals make better parents, simply because they gain a greater understanding and thus a greater respect for the new life.

Some of the salutary effects of "getting the picture" are illustrated by a study undertaken some years ago by Dr. Stewart Campbell of the University of London and Anthony Reading, a clinical psychologist. Women who were shown ultrasound images of their fetuses, these researchers discovered, were far more likely to stop smoking and abstain from alcohol during pregnancy than women who didn't see such pictures.

Psychologist Reading, in collaboration with Dr. Larry Platt of the Los Angeles County-University of Southern California Medical Center, is making a further study of mother-fetus bonding, using ultrasound images. "Early bonding," Dr. Platt told the *Los Angeles Times* recently, "helps to put into parents' minds the fact that the fetus is a patient and that they, the parents, must take care of themselves better."[2] Using ultrasound pictures, he added, "brings the father into the

[2]Quoted in the *San Francisco Chronicle* (March 7, 1983):15.

pregnancy, too. He often gets more excited about the picture than the mother does."

Of course, we should not base decisions of what is human and what is not human entirely on what our eyes tell us. We owe it to ourselves to use all our senses and the full force of our reasoning faculties. The essence of humanity is *not* perfect bilateral symmetry, baby-blue eyes, dimples, and a fetching smile. We have to search deeper than that to find the real basis of humanity. There are biological realities more impressive, more awesome, and even more beautiful in some ways than that first ultrasound image of the baby in the womb. The events that create that first cell, that single-celled human being, are no less extraordinary than the "finished product" itself.

Before we try to see what the picture looks like in its totality, let's find out what it's made of.

In the Beginning

Most of the billions of cells that collectively make up a human being are "soma" (Greek for "body") cells. Unless manipulated in exotic ways, these body cells are and remain just what they appear to be: skin, hair, bone, muscle, and so on. Each has some worthy, special function in life, a function that it dutifully, if narrowly, performs until it dies. And the soma cells *do* die, ultimately leaving nothing of themselves behind.

There are some other, far rarer cells, however,—known as "germ" cells or "sex" cells—that have the power not only to extravagantly transform themselves, giving rise to *every* other kind of human cell, but also to seize for themselves a bit of the "impossible": immortality. The sex cells are the sperm cells in the male and the egg cells in the female. It is only in combination, one with the other, that these cells can work their special magic, rise above the humdrum stasis of their somatic siblings, and confer something of their essences upon the future generations in which they will thus perpetuate themselves.

There is an "essence" in every cell, whether somatic or germinal, consisting of the nucleic acids, principally deoxyribonucleic acid—better known as "DNA," the basic stuff that forms the "building blocks" of life, the genes and chromosomes. Actually the genes are made up of much smaller units, so numerous that if you were by some miracle able to completely "unravel" the strands of DNA that exist in a single human being the "chain of life" would stretch across some millions of miles. There are many thousands of genes in the nucleus (central core) of each cell; these are arranged in larger chromosomal units, of which there are forty-six in each human body cell. The individual sex cells, sperm and egg, on the other hand, contain only half that number: twenty-three chromosomes each. It is only through combination, through merger, that the sex cells attain the full complement of hereditary units that defines a human being.

Why should an egg cell that has merged with a sperm cell be regarded as "human life," as a "person," when in fact it contains exactly the same genetic combination, precisely the same chromosomal pattern that each of trillions of ordinary body cells that make up skin, bone, etc., will contain? Before I answer that question and explore the remarkable events that occur when the sex cells *do* combine, let us understand something more of the origins and behavior of the sex cells in their "single" (noncombined) state. That behavior is, at the very least, remarkable.

The Serene Ovum: "Queen Mother" of Cells

There *is* something serene, almost regal, about the ovum (the egg cell). The shape itself—a sphere—suggests great calm and perhaps potential perfection. I sometimes call the ovum "the queen mother of us all." Like queen ants and queen bees, this queen-of-the-cells is a giant of heroic—perhaps one should say heroinelike—proportions, at least when compared with most other cells in the human body. The ovum weighs in, at the height of its powers, at 1/20th of a *millionth* of an ounce. Its majestic girth (diameter) is about 1/175th of an inch. As befits a royal presence, the ovum moves at a leisurely pace, particulary when contrasted with its frantic counterpart, the sperm cell, a puny but potent whippet that weighs only about 1/90,000th as much. The mature ovum, moreover, is attended by a lavish court, surrounded by thousands of lesser cells—what I call protective "ladies-in-waiting"—each one of which had a chance to become a queen but for various reasons was passed by and reduced to an also-ran.

By the time a female child is born, she already has more than a million primitive egg cells in her ovaries. So important are these cells in the ongoing struggle for survival (perpetuation of the human species) that the egg cells are among the first to form when a new female life begins to take shape in the womb. Three weeks after conception, the human embryo produces one hundred or so primitive egg cells which migrate, as if they had minds of their own, to the location at which the ovaries, the female sex glands, will form. These cells take up residence in the developing ovaries and rapidly multiply until there are millions of them in mid-pregnancy. After that, it's all downhill in terms of numbers. By the time the child becomes a woman, she has only a few hundred thousand primary egg cells left, the rest having succumbed to stress, strain, and the normal maturation process. Of those that do survive only a relative few—about 400—grow to the point where they become real candidates for "coronation"—that is, fertilization.

At puberty the pituitary gland in the brain sets in motion a complex series of events by secreting hormones which in turn affect other glands in the body. Under the influence of these hormonal currents, the girl's body develops into that of a woman, and the female reproductive (menstrual) cycle begins. The average cycle is twenty-eight days long, with ovulation—the release from the ovary of a mature egg cell—occurring about midway through the cycle, near Day 14. The ovum bursts out of a follicle that protrudes from the surface of the ovary. At this point the egg is surrounded by more than 5,000 "nurse" cells, the "ladies-in-waiting." These protective cells form the "corona radiata," a shimmering halo of cells that not only protects the egg but adds mass to it, making it easier for it to be "picked up" by the hovering fimbriae (thin, finger-like projections) of the fallopian tube, through which the egg must pass if it is to rendezvous with the sperm and ultimately reach the womb.

If the egg is not fertilized by a sperm cell (that is, does not merge with a sperm cell) within hours of ovulation, all is lost for that particular would-be queen. The hormonal processes that cause the egg to ripen and emerge from the ovarian follicle have also been "priming" the womb, getting it ready to receive the egg in the event that it is fertilized in the tube. These hormones nourish the lining of the womb, thickening and enriching it so that it becomes fertile ground for "nesting" by a newly fertilized egg—which is, in fact, a new human being. If the egg is "disappointed," and no sperm shows up to add its complement of chromosomes to the egg's, then the "bed" that has been prepared for it—the lining of the womb—is stripped away and expelled through the process of menstruation, during what most women call their "period."

Thereafter the cycle starts over again, with yet another "hopeful" emerging from the ovary at midcycle. If an egg is eventually fertilized and implants itself in the succulent lining of the uterus, the ovarian follicle from which it issued is also preserved. It remains active in the ovary in order to help maintain the newly established pregnancy. It does this by producing hormones that sustain the "receptivity" of the uterine lining; it also prevents other eggs from maturing, events that would disrupt and terminate the pregnancy already in progress.

Sperm Cells: They Risk All to Be "The One"

The male child at birth already possesses some millions of primitive sperm cells. As in the case of the female, these sex cells have migrated to the site of the developing sex glands—the testes in the case of the male—very early in the life of the embryo. These primitive cells remain dormant inside the convoluted tubules of the testes until puberty, when the pituitary gland secretes hormones that cause the boy to assume the deeper voice, beard, and other physical characteristics of the mature male. The events of puberty also cause the primitive

31

sex cells to mature and give rise to still more sperm cells, at the rate of approximately 300 million per day.

A healthy mature male may ejaculate up to five cubic centimeters of seminal fluid in one sexual climax. Each cubic centimeter of this fluid may contain as many as 300 million vigorous spermatozoa (mature sperm cells); thus, the male *may* unleash more than *one billion* spermatozoa at one time, all aimed at *one egg*! Since it takes only one sperm to fertilize an egg, what could possibly account for this apparent "overkill"? Did God or Mother Nature make a massive mistake?

Not really. The egg is quite a formidable entity compared with the tiny sperm cell. You could put all the eggs that were required to create the entire world population today into a single cookie jar; the sperm required for that same job would fill no more than a thimble. Though sperm are longer than eggs are wide (a typical sperm is about 1/500th of an inch long), almost all that length is accounted for by a narrow, whiplike tail. The head of the sperm, which contains its nucleus and therefore its chromosomes, is only a tiny fraction of the size and volume of the egg. Not only are the diminutive spermatozoa given the task of penetrating a massive target with what amounts to a "thick hide," but they also have to get to that target through an obstacle course that can only be described as "killing." Most of the sperm never get anywhere near the object of their frenzied affections. They not only risk all, but almost always "give all" in the effort to be "the one" sperm that will unite with the egg to create a new human life. Their enormous numbers help ensure that at least one sperm *will* reach the egg.

I sometimes liken the sperm's task of getting to the egg—across the space of six to eleven inches, through part of the vaginal canal, into the cervix, through the uterus, and up the fallopian tube—to that faced by a spawning salmon which has to swim upstream against a rushing current for many miles. Actually the mission is far more formidable than even that suggests, for not only do the sperm have to swim "upstream," but they also have to withstand the acid environment into which they are abruptly thrust when they enter the vagina. Unlike the well-protected, well-nourished egg, the sperm cell enters the world outside the testes "stripped to the shorts," as I sometimes explain it to my patients. It operates on the bare essentials and is designed more for speed and maneuverability than for staying power. The sperm has to get to the egg and get there quickly or die. It carries with it very little in the way of excess "energy reserves" and has little to protect it against a hostile environment.

Sperm rarely survive for more than forty-eight hours inside the female. Most survive for only a few hours; many in fact die very quickly in the relatively acidic milieu of the vagina, never making it any further. I discovered years ago that female secretions become increasingly alkaline as ovulation approaches, but even then, the vaginal environment remains threatening. Those sperm cells that are propelled to the back of the vagina and into or near the cervix, the opening of the womb, are likely to do better than those that lag behind. The outflowing cervical secretions are more favorable to sperm than those of the vagina, but the outflow is just that—a sticky swirl that must be crossed. Those that get through the cervix and into the uterus face easier going, at least for a while. Having got to the back of the uterus, however, a great many sperm will "choose" the wrong fallopian tube, the one leading to the ovary that *didn't* release an egg that month.

Even those sperm that chance to select the "correct" channel must now redouble their efforts, whipping their tails as hard as they can to fight their way against the same current that is carrying the calm, cool, and unexercised egg *downstream*. This "current" consists of the muscular contractions of the tubal walls, the "ciliary" beating of tiny, hairlike cells, and the downward streaming of fluid. Many of the sperm cells will run into one of thousands of little culs-de-sac or blind alleys off the main channel of the tube and burn themselves out literally knocking their heads against walls. As if this were not bad enough, female white blood cells, scavengers of the woman's immunity system, may sweep down like monsters in a video game and gobble up the sperm cells just as they would any other "foreign body" or "invader."

Perhaps all these obstacles are designed to see to it that **33** only the most "worthy"—that is, the "fittest"—has any chance of becoming the egg's consort. It seems certain, however, that at least some luck is also essential. There are differing viewpoints on what happens when the hardy band of surviving sperm get close to the egg. My own test-tube observations show that some sperm may still miss the target, perhaps by only a hair, charging right on by. I tend to doubt what some others have claimed, namely, that the egg exerts some attracting force that draws the survivors to "her." Whatever the case, only hundreds or a few thousand may actually make contact with the egg, and then *only one* will be admitted inside.

The "Dance of Love" and Conception

Under ideal conditions it may take the sperm "front runners" a couple hours—sometimes less—to get to the egg and begin the fertilization process. That's provided the egg is in the tube when the sperm arrive there. If ovulation has not yet occurred, the sperm will have to "cool their heels," wait around, and hope for the best. Many will die waiting. But even if the egg does not arrive for a day or two, there *may* yet be some hardy fellows standing by and still energetic enough to do the job. The chances for this, however, decrease as the wait increases.

Assuming an ideal rendezvous, a few thousand sperm cells may meet the egg, usually in the upper third of the fallopian tube, each boring into the protective outer layer, fighting for admission into the egg's inner sanctum. At this point the egg has shed some of its "nurse" cells, making entry somewhat easier. There is still a tough membrane around the egg, however, and this too must be penetrated before the sperm can get to the egg nucleus and there merge with its chromosomes. This membrane, the "zona pellucida," is a clear, gelatinous barrier.

Fortunately, each sperm has more than just its whiplike tail to help it dig into the egg. It also comes equipped with a "cap" or "nose cone" called the "acrosome." The acrosome

34

contains a chemical, an enzyme called hyaluronidase, that helps dissolve the egg's protective layers and thus makes entry easier. As the sperm bore into the egg's zona pellucida, they beat their tails synchronously, creating a wave effect that looks like grass undulating in the wind. The effect of this is to cause the egg to rotate, quite rapidly in some instances and always in the clockwise direction. I have dubbed this spectacle "the dance of love."

It is not known for certain whether the *first* sperm to make contact with the egg is the one that will be admitted inside the egg; it is probably one of the first to make contact. In any event, once a single sperm penetrates the zona pellucida, changes occur in the egg membrane that prevent all other sperm cells from getting through, no matter how long and how hard they try to do so. And they *do* keep trying, whipping their tails until they die of exhaustion, continuing to spin the egg in the process, an activity that does them no good but may still benefit the newly fertilized egg by causing it to move more quickly down the tube toward the womb.

The "winning" sperm penetrates, tail and all, through the egg membrane, entering the clear protoplasmic outer portion of the egg (the "cytoplasm"). This occurrence, apart from "shutting the door" on all other sperm, sets up a violent vibration within the egg cytoplasm. The sperm presence stimulates the final maturation of the egg which, in the midst of all this turbulence, expels excess nuclear material in the form of a "polar body." The sperm loses its "nose cone" and also its tail as it moves into the center of the egg. Finally the sperm is reduced to its "pro-nucleus," a package of twenty-three chromosomes. The sperm pro-nucleus approaches and then makes contact with the egg's pro-nucleus. I have observed a definite attractive force at work here that draws the two nuclear spheres together. The nuclear envelopes seem to dissolve at the point of contact, and the twenty-three chromosomes from each of the pro-nuclei are free at last to merge, first condensing and grouping together, then forming into pairs with one member coming from each donor. Thus it is that each parent contributes an equal number of chromosomes to the new life.

35

The merger is complete within twelve hours, at which time the egg—which may have "waited" as many as forty years for this moment—is fertilized and becomes known technically as the "zygote," containing the full set of forty-six chromosomes required to create new human life. Conception has occurred. The genotype—the inherited characteristics of a unique human being—is established in the conception process and will remain in force for the entire life of that individual. No other event in biological life is so decisive as this one; no other set of circumstances can even remotely rival genotype in "making you what you are."

Conception confers life and makes that life one of a kind. Unless you have an identical twin, there is virtually no chance, in the natural course of things, that there will ever be "another you"—not even if mankind were to persist for billions of years. Indeed, given the vast number of combinations possible among chromosomes, genes, and their smaller subparts, there is virtually no chance that even your own parents could ever come up with another "copy" of you, not even if by some magic they could produce millions of offspring.

The power of genotype can scarcely be overestimated. Your genetic makeup—established the moment fertilization is completed and conception occurs—determines not only your physical characteristics, but also—more powerfully than anything else that can be demonstrated—how you will process information, how you will think, what you will *be* in what we call "mind." Studies of identical twins separated at or near birth and then reunited through happenstance later in life have proved how powerfully genotype shapes not only one's physical characteristics but also one's mental outlook, tastes, opinions, habits, and psychological predispositions. Environment is by no means the only or even the most important shaper of behavior.

Many who have studied the data regarding twins have declared themselves awed and astounded by the evident, sometimes overwhelming power of heredity. Even twins who have grown up in radically different home environments have exhibited, upon observation in later life, astonishing behavioral similarities. A significant number are found to have adopted remarkably similar lifestyles, often choosing the same occupations, marrying women who are alike in too many particulars to be accounted for by coincidence alone, and so on. The genotype that is conferred at conception does not merely start life, it *defines* life.

Conception sets in motion a series of events within the womb more complex and wondrous than anything that will ever happen to the body outside the womb. So astonishing are the happenings that transpire in the first moments, days, weeks, and months of life-before-birth that when we come to understand them fully we will very likely possess the answer to such puzzles as cancer and the aging process. By fully understanding life we will almost certainly be able to better understand death.

Between Fertilization and Implantation

The next several chapters are devoted to the progress of the new life in the womb. For the moment, let us return to the fertilized egg still moving, perhaps a little more quickly now, down the fallopian tube. The tube itself is more than just a simple conduit. As the fertilized egg begins to divide and grow, the tube provides nourishment and protection. Even before the zygote undergoes its first cleavage (division), its sex has been determined. It is the sperm, not the egg, that decides the matter of sex. The egg always contributes an X sex chromosome; sperm cells may contribute either an X or a Y sex chromosome. If a Y-bearing sperm merges with an egg, the resulting combination is XY, which means a boy has been conceived. If an X-bearing sperm fertilizes the egg, the resulting combination is XX, which means a girl has been conceived.

It is worth noting in passing that X and Y sperm behave somewhat differently. I have found that the smaller Y-bearing (boy-producing) sperm are faster but less resistant to biochemical stress than their larger, hardier X-bearing (girl-producing) brothers. These observations have become the basis for various methods to *preselect* the sex of one's offspring.

37

Human development proceeds from the single-cell state to the multi-cell state through the self-replication of the DNA molecules that exist within the original fertilized egg cell. The cell in effect copies itself, dividing in half as its chromosomes duplicate themselves and form new nuclei. The new cells in turn divide, and the cell mass grows ever more rapidly. Each new cell is an identical copy of the original, for each cell contains exactly the same chromosomal combination as the original fertilized egg cell. Given this exact sameness, how is it possible for these cells to make up all the *different* tissues of the body? That is a question I will answer in the next chapter.

The first cell cleavage takes place within thirty-six hours of fertilization, with subsequent divisions requiring considerably less time. Normally the cells hold together after this first division. Sometimes, however, the first two cells split apart and begin dividing separately, thus giving rise to *identical twins*. (Fraternal—non-identical—twins, on the other hand, arise when two different eggs are fertilized by separate sperm, something that can happen when the ovaries release more than one mature egg at a time. "Identical twins" are genetically identical; fraternal twins are not.)

My test-tube studies show that as cell division continues and accelerates, the individual cells become more closely associated with each other. By the time the fertilized egg reaches the womb, it will have grown to a mass of sixteen or more cells integrated into a mulberry-shaped sphere called a "morula." It usually takes about three days for the morula to reach the womb. Then for the next two to three days it may move freely about in the uterus, growing to the "blastula" or blastocyst stage, assuming a hollow shape made up of sixty or more cells.

At this point the cells have already begun to differentiate, some gathering at one side of the spherical mass to prepare for the further development of the human embryo while other cells take different positions to prepare to provide protective cover and support systems for the new life. The different layers of cells which have formed around the hollow space in the middle of the irregularly shaped sphere, moreover, are already being assigned specific tasks—the development of the brain and nervous system, the stomach, the liver, and so on. Still other cells are organized to begin digging into the uterine lining in order to establish a "lifeline" with the mother. The next chapter begins at this point: implantation in the uterine wall.

Back to the Question: *Is* There Life Before Conception?

Fascinating and purposeful though the sex cells are, ova and spermatozoa do *not* by themselves constitute human life. The sex cells are "half worlds" which only become whole in combination with each other—through the process I have described. This process helps to ensure, through its nearly infinite recombinant genetic possibilities, the continued variability, adaptability, and development of the species. In returning to the opening question, it may seem that I am belaboring the obvious; but the question does have some bearing on the abortion debate.

Some pro-abortionists of the "life-is-a-continuum" school of thought have attempted to belittle the significance of the human zygote (fertilized egg), claiming it is no more worthy to be considered human life than is a single egg or sperm cell. Indeed, some go so far as to claim that if you can call the zygote human life, then you can call every other cell in the body human life as well.

John D. Biggers of Harvard Medical School states, for example:

> As far as humans are concerned, we can speak of both diploid and haploid individuals, referring to these individuals at different stages of the life cycle as ovum, spermatozoon, zygote, embryo, fetus, girl, boy, woman, man. . . . So to suggest that life begins with a particular stage—the zygote, for example, . . . is foolish.[3]

It is by such arguments that some pro-abortionists try to back the other side into a corner, claiming that if you are going to

---

[3] *The Sciences* (December 1981).

protect the zygote, then you are obligated to protect the sex cells as well, an obvious impossibility.

There may be some arguing in this fashion who earnestly believe that they have perceived a chink in the anti-abortion position, but most, I am convinced, are being disingenuous. They know full well that there is a world of difference between a haploid sex cell and a diploid zygote. Only the zygote possesses a unique human genotype and the power of full differentiation, a power without which no human life can be expressed. The haploid sex cells are *parts of potential human life*. The zygote *is* human life.

There is another argument sometimes raised by the pro-abortionists that should be dealt with here. The fact that a significant number of zygotes fail to implant and therefore do not result in pregnancy is seized upon by a few as "evidence" that "even Mother Nature" does not consider the fertilized egg genuine human life, any more than "she" does the hundreds of thousands of eggs and millions of sperm that are "wasted." To this I can only answer that there are also a significant number of one-year-old infants who will never make it to old age, to puberty, or even to their second birthdays. Does the fact that life is interrupted at some point after it has begun mean that it never existed?

2

Making Contact

Implantation and the First Month of Life

Putting Down Roots (Under Water)

The blastocyst, comprising as many as two hundred cells, begins to attach itself to the uterine lining six or seven days after fertilization. Where it attaches itself to the uterus may be determined in part by the mother's sleeping habits. My research has shown, for example, that women who sleep supine—on their backs—are most likely to have babies that have affixed themselves to the posterior wall of the uterus. This can be of more than merely academic interest in cases where delivery will have to be by Caesarean section. The blastocyst does its "digging" by way of invasive cells called "trophoblast." These put out extensions that insinuate their way into the endometrium. Enzymes released by the trophoblast cells may also assist in the "nesting" or "digging in" process.

Implantation is not achieved in a matter of minutes or hours. It is a process that continues for several weeks. Nevertheless, the embryo begins to derive nourishment from the mother almost immediately. It does this by soaking up nutrients from small blood vessels that burst as it digs into the uterine wall. So rich are these nutrients that for several days,

41

the embryo more than doubles in size every twenty-four hours. The invasive trophoblast, meanwhile, serve another function: They act as an immunological barrier between embryo and mother so that neither will try to reject the other as foreign. This complex task appears to be largely under the control of the embryo rather than the mother.

Well-nourished though the embryo is during the first few days after implantation begins, continued development depends on the placenta, an organ of such complexity that man, for all his technological ingenuity, has never created anything that can remotely compare with it. The placenta forms where the trophoblast digs into the uterine wall. It begins developing in the earliest stages of implantation, arising out of the trophoblast, and goes on developing and changing throughout most of pregnancy, constantly accommodating the needs of the new life.

At time of birth, the placenta may cover half the uterine wall and weigh well over a pound. It is a disc-shaped mass of tissue richly interlaced with capillaries (tiny blood vessels) and a few larger vessels, all of which link mother and baby, collectively acting as "go-between" and "exchange center." The placenta is like a complex, computerized filter through which hormones and various nutrients may pass to the embryo and through which waste materials may be carried away and the blood purified. The placenta serves many of the functions that the baby's internal organs—liver, kidneys, lungs, and so on—will assume as they develop later on.

The placenta has a maternal side as well as an embryonic/fetal side. It is not a set of simple pipes through which blood flows into the unborn, as some may imagine. In fact, there is very little intermingling of the mother's blood with that of the baby: The new life produces its own blood. The mother's system removes wastes from the baby's blood and supplies it with nutrients and fresh oxygen. The stagnant blood of the unborn is carried into the placenta—and re-oxygenated blood returned therefrom—via the umbilical cord. The semi-permeable nature of the placental tissues and vessels enables molecules to pass selectively between mother and baby.

It is becoming increasingly apparent to me that a variety of complex biochemicals may pass through the placenta, some sending signals to the baby, some to the mother. As I will discuss in more detail later, the unborn may thus "sense" not only the mother's physical status, but even her mental status and her attitudes to some extent. Anger, for example, and other manifestations of stress have clearly been linked to biochemical changes that may affect development in the womb. The unborn can send out "distress signals" when something is wrong, alerting the mother and her doctor to some peril. The mother may confer limited immunity to various diseases upon her baby via placental exchange. The placenta itself controls some of the hormonal events of pregnancy; it seems to know when to switch itself off and thus help start labor at the end.

Like the placenta, the amniotic sac, or "bag of waters," in which the baby will grow for approximately nine months begins forming almost as soon as implantation begins. And the amniotic membrane likewise arises out of the trophoblast. It gradually surrounds the embryo and fills with fluid that serves, among other things, as a shock absorber. Eventually there will be about a quart of fluid in the sac. The fluid is warm, clear, and mildly alkaline. It buffers the baby and prevents it from sticking to things during its rapid growth and development. It also enables free movement and acrobatics later on in pregnancy. Kicking, swimming, and even flipping over in this watery home, the baby practices some of the motions and movements that will be useful in the life "outside."

The amniotic fluid also helps to maintain proper body temperature and occasionally provides a little extra nutrition, since it contains various sugars and proteins. At one point in its development, the unborn swallows as many as several pints of amniotic fluid a day. I have discovered that if sugars are *added* to the fluid, the baby will drink even more of it; but if something bitter is added, consumption decreases rapidly. The unborn will also urinate into the fluid; yet it does not become "polluted," for it is purified via recycling through the maternal system several times a day. By analyzing cells that slough off the fetus into the amniotic fluid, doctors can, at a certain point in pregnancy, diagnose the sex of the unborn child and in some instances detect a variety of genetic abnormalities.

Development and Differentiation:
Cells That "Talk" and "Travel"

After the high drama of conception and the necessity of nest-making comes the full frenzy of development. This seemingly chaotic process can be seen, on close examination, to possess elegant, even *miraculous* order. People who argue that the zygote is "only a blueprint" and that "a blueprint is not the same as a building" are teetering on a groundless analogy: We would have to regard it as an architectural blueprint which, left to its own devices and in the natural order of things, will spontaneously and with amazing speed give rise not merely to an edifice but to a megalopolis the likes of which we have never seen on earth. Obviously, no mere blueprint can achieve all that.

During the first month, the new human life increases its size fortyfold; by the end of pregnancy, its weight will increase an estimated six-billionfold. From the one-celled zygote there will arise billions of cells, each of which must assume its rightful place and function, creating an integrated whole capable of making muscle and music and other expressions of "mind"—a self-constructing, self-organizing process of differentiation that astounds researchers on the leading edge of molecular and cell biology.

In studying the mysteries of development and differentiation we are approaching some of the fundamental secrets of life. These secrets, once unlocked, will help us to understand better not only the *schedule* of our creation, but also the *schemata* of it. These schemata will surely tell us important things both about how cells "go right" and about how they "go wrong," providing us with new approaches to treating cancer, genetic diseases, perhaps aging itself. We have already begun to learn the "language of life" by deciphering part of the genetic code. But we still need to know much more about how cells intercommunicate, how they "talk" to each other, how they "know" what to become and where to situate themselves in a complex structure.

The instructions for making a whole new human being are bound up in the chromosomes and genes of the first cell— the zygote. But how do those instructions get expressed? How do all the cells that spring from the original become so *different* when, in fact, they all contain the same set of instructions? What makes one become a liver cell, for example, and another a brain cell?

This process of *differentiation* is at the heart of what we call "development." It is apparent that there is some method by which *most* of the instructions in each cell are *switched off*— that is, are non-functioning—once differentiation gets under way. Each body cell contains all the instructions needed to make *all* parts of the body. Obviously, if all those instructions were switched on, there would be runaway growth with no organization or meaningful development. It is only when cells divide up the labor and express only the right portions of their billions of instructions for making up specific parts that meaningful development can occur.

Only recently have researchers begun to understand how cells "know" what to become. Our understanding is still sketchy, but some tantalizing insights are emerging. It is beginning to appear that the genes do not, in the strictest sense, do all the directing. It seems that when a certain number of cells congregate, they begin passing messages among themselves. The cells seem to me to be influenced in their behavior by the company they keep. When things get too crowded in one area, for example, some cells simply take off for the "frontier," to new areas of development—to the site, for example, of a future liver, sex gland, or finger. Some cells are better frontiersmen than others, though why this is we still do not know.

In any event, in studies of animal embryos, cell movement can be traced from one point to another. The "explorers" make a path through the other cells by releasing enzymes that help clear the way. Groups of outward-bound cells, all somehow of the same mind, move to specific areas along "roadways" made of supportive proteins and sugars. When they get to where they want to settle, the enzyme secretions cease, forward movement stops, and organ formation begins.

Equally remarkable is the fact that when a variety of cells which have begun to show early signs of differentiation are mixed together in laboratory cultures, "like-minded" cells will *unmix* themselves and gradually find their compatriots, clumping together within the culture. In other words, cells that had begun to differentiate as liver cells will find other newly emerging liver cells, brain cells will find other brain cells, and so on. This shows that there are forces at work that ensure that only certain cells will travel and settle down together, for the purpose of making specific organs or other bodily structures.

Once a particular organ is under development, however, it appears that the site itself becomes all-important in determining what a cell that arrives there will do. It is clear that cells in groups possess something that cells by themselves do not. Or perhaps it is simply *more* of something, a biochemical and/or bioelectrical synergy or set of synergies. Whatever the case, if I transplant a cell from a liver-making colony to the site of a kidney-under-construction, the errant liver cell will soon give up its old identity and become one of the fellows, i.e., just another kidney cell.

It has been demonstrated that molecules within the complex biochemical matrix that holds cells together can effect the function of individual cells, determining which of their genes will switch on and off. It is possible, therefore, that not only the embryonic environment, but even the maternal environment may affect development in some cases. Faulty biochemical signals may lead to the same kinds of disordered differentiation that give rise to cancers and to various birth defects. There are striking similarities between roving embryonic cells and runaway cancer cells; my recent observations reveal that they follow some of the same migratory patterns and exhibit some of the same invasive behavior.

Other theories are emerging to further explain the selective expression of genetic instructions within cells. Perhaps there are "repressor" molecules that control these events; per-

46

haps there are specific genes in each cell that are the "switch-masters." Whatever the case, it is evident that the search for a solution to these fundamental puzzles of life will benefit all of us. For the present, I cannot do other than agree with one researcher in this field, biologist Laurie Iten of Purdue University, who has been quoted as saying, "We believe that cells talk to each other. They aren't dumb." There is a method in what first seems to be the "madness" or chaos of development—a method so inventive, so marvelous, that any who even begin to plumb the depths of its mysteries cannot but be awed. Here, surely, is life that is purposeful and meaningful.

Emergence of the Heart and the Nervous System

Before the first month of life is over, the embryo has already developed a beating heart and put down the foundations of its nervous system, including brain, nerves, and spinal cord. The eyes have begun to develop, as have most of the major organs. A "yolk sac" begins to form soon after implantation that will produce the embryo's red blood cells until its liver, spleen, and bone marrow become functional. The yolk sac also gives rise to the primitive sex cells that will migrate into the developing ovaries and testes during the second month. The placenta grows rapidly during the first month, as does the embryo itself, attaining a crown-to-rump (sitting) height of nearly a quarter-inch by the thirtieth day of life. The "rump" at this point is more like a tail, which disappears later on.

Though the eyes, ears, and nose have begun to form by the end of the first month, the embryo is still without easily recognizable facial features. Its head is large, accounting for more than half of its total body length, and it is tucked downward, seemingly resting on a bulge in the chest. This bulge can be seen to pulsate, for it surrounds the embryonic heart, which is already pumping blood manufactured in the yolk sac. Arms and legs are represented at this point by small buds.

Perhaps the most significant development in the first month is the brain and the nervous system. A groove along the back of the embryo begins closing up in the third week to form a tube, providing a channel for the spinal cord. The brain begins to form at the top of this neural tube; all three of its major areas are demarcated by the end of the first month. Primitive nerve fiber begins branching out from the brain and spinal cord, reaching into all parts of the embryo's rapidly forming body. The development of the brain and nervous system may begin almost as soon as the egg is fertilized and continue on even several weeks after birth.

So rapid is development in the first month, as one cell becomes millions, that all the major structures of the body are in evidence, though not yet finished by any means, by the thirtieth day. The important muscle groups are all in place, and the building blocks of the spinal column are stacked up. The mouth is capable of opening by the twenty-eighth day, providing access to a still incomplete digestive system. Liver cells begin congregating in one place by the twenty-first day, and a recognizable liver is detectable by the thirtieth. The so-called gill-arches—folds which make the embryo look as if it has double or triple chins—are preparing to become the jaws, ears, and various internal throat structures.

To Have or Have Not: Pregnancy or Abortion?

The embryo is already likely to have a beating heart by the time its mother begins to suspect that she is pregnant. The missed menstrual period alerts the woman to the possibility of pregnancy. There are some special tests that can detect pregnancy even *before* a missed period, though the kinds of tests most women will find readily available are not reliable until about two weeks after the missed period.

Women who choose to have abortions very early in pregnancy may select a method of killing the embryo that is called "menstrual extraction," a technique that is now much in decline but was once enthusiastically embraced by some feminists. It is, in fact, still listed in some current texts on abortion. See, for example, *Abortion: Health Care Perspectives* by E. Dorsey Smith, assistant director of nursing in the Maternal-Child Division of Mt. Sinai Medical Center in New York

City.[1] Dr. Smith refers to menstrual extraction as "minabortion" and notes that it is "the removal of the contents of the uterus within five to fourteen days after a missed period."

Actually, the method has been used in some instances within hours after a woman merely suspects that she is beginning to miss or *might* miss her period. Some women were attracted to menstrual extraction because they could use it without being certain that they were pregnant. I call this relieving oneself of guilt through self-deception.

Some doctors have been all too willing to administer this method, deepening the deception by saying that menstrual extraction is simply being used to "regularize" a woman's cycle, as if it had failed to arrive only by chance and not because of pregnancy.

Menstrual extraction is carried out by inserting a small cannula into the womb, through the vagina and cervix. The contents of the womb are then sucked out by hand, simply by squeezing an ampulla attached to the cannula.

But the idea of menstrual extraction is unwise and the procedure for it unsafe. A missed period could be due to something other than pregnancy. A woman who believes that pregnancy is the reason for her irregularity may obtain a false sense of security from extraction, for the lack of bleeding may in fact be caused by a tumor or some other potentially serious disorder, which then goes unheeded and undetected for a time. The cannula, moreover, though it looks innocent, can be difficult to handle and has been known to cause serious perforations of the uterus.

It is worth noting that the "father of menstrual extraction" was Harvey Karman, a man who, in the early 1970s, was a favorite not only of those who liked to think of themselves as "radical feminists," but also of an impressive array of pro-abortion forces. The Karman cannula and menstrual extraction, according to the rhetoric of that time, were about to revolutionize efforts to control world population, place women further in control of their bodies, and make abortion safe, simple, and cheap enough for everyone. An article in

[1](New York: Appleton-Century Crofts, 1982).

the *Los Angeles Times* treated Karman very favorably and identified him as "doctor." Apparently he had the respect of the International Planned Parenthood Federation and the National Women's Health Coalition which jointly helped him go to Bangladesh with the blessings of the United Nations. There Karman and his team of "paramedics" were to administer abortions to women raped by invading Pakistanis.

Had the *Los Angeles Times,* Planned Parenthood, and the U.N. bothered to check, they would have discovered that the college from which Karman claimed to have received his degree was not even a degree-granting institution. Karman possessed neither the M.D. nor the Ph.D. degrees that he claimed to have. Worse, since 1953 there had been *nine* felony charges filed against him, ranging from grand theft to murder. The murder charge proceeded from the death of a woman he had aborted with a nutcracker in a motel room; he was acquitted of murder in that case, but found guilty of illegal abortion. He served more than two years in prison on that and theft charges. Numerous other charges have been filed against him in recent years. In 1979 he was arrested for performing five illegal abortions and practicing medicine without a license. His only genuine degree, it turns out, was in theatrical arts.

3

Humanity at Under One Ounce
The Second and Third Months

Purpose at One Ounce

Before we follow the embryo/fetus through the next two months of its life, let's take a quick look ahead to see where the adventure leads. The end of the third month marks the conclusion of what many doctors, as a matter of convenience, call the "first trimester," the first third of pregnancy. By the end of this trimester the embryo will be called a "fetus." It will have easily recognized facial features, will exceed three inches in length, and weigh about an ounce. The fetus will be capable of movements and expressions that are distinctly its own, the product of inheritance from mother and father, shaped to some extent by the environment in the womb.

Activity is far from merely random by the end of the first trimester. There is *purpose* in what the fetus does. It is already practicing for life outside the womb. Brain development is sufficiently advanced that the fetus can react to touch, turn its head, kick its legs, flex its wrists, make fists, and even curl its toes. It also sucks its thumb and swallows amniotic fluid, getting ready for the day when it will have something more substantial to consume. It practices breathing, even though it still has no air; using features that are now distinctly babylike, the fetus begins to perfect some of the facial expressions by which it will later let its parents know its moods, its likes, and its dislikes.

It should be understood that though I use different terms to describe the unborn—*zygote, embryo, fetus*—these labels do not reflect distinctly different phases of development; these terms are used as a matter of convenience to describe general changes. Some describe the "zygote" as becoming the "embryo" at the time of implantation; others say the "embryo stage" begins in the third week of pregnancy. Some say the "fetal stage" begins in the fifth week of development; others say the eighth week, and still others say the embryo does not become the fetus until the end of the first trimester. It is my view that once the major processes of differentiation are largely complete, the embryo becomes the fetus. That occurs by the end of the eighth week.

Whatever the terminology, the unborn is *always* a distinct entity, an individual human life in its own right and not simply some "disposable part of the mother's body," as some pro-abortionists argue. Fetologist Albert W. Liley has asserted: "It is the fetus who is in charge of the pregnancy." Even some who oppose restrictions on abortion would readily agree. For example, Daniel Callahan, director of the Institute of Society, Ethics and the Life Sciences, has stated: "Genetically, hormonally and in all organic respects save for the source of its nourishment, a fetus and even an embryo is separate from the woman."

The Second Month

Let us look now at some of the highlights of development through the end of the second month of life, as the major differentiation processes are completed and the embryo makes the transition to fetus:

The Fifth Week. The embryo weighs only 1/1000th of an ounce and is about one-third-inch "tall," crown-to-rump; leg and arm buds are becoming prominent, and by the end of the fifth week, the gross outline of the hands—with fingers appearing webbed—is evident. The jaw has begun to form, giving the face some recognizable appearance. Lung buds are present, and the windpipe is forming, along with the stomach, esophagus, and various visceral organs. The sex cells are on the move, as described earlier. The cerebral cortex of the brain, responsible for the higher thinking processes and meaningful movement of the body, is taking shape. The brain stem is soon recognizable. Muscle groups are in place, and the embryo may already be capable of movement, though not to the extent that the mother can detect such movements.

The Sixth Week. The external ears are appearing, and the limbs are becoming more fully developed. Foot plates are in evidence—with the webbed look—while the hand plates may now have progressed so that fingers are distinctly separate from one another. Even as the limbs become more prominent, the tail becomes less so, regressing slowly. Several important glands, including the pituitary and the thyroid, are present and developing rapidly. The sex cells reach the areas in which the sex glands themselves are forming. The gill arches disappear, pigmented eyes are visible through a translucent covering of skin, the yolk sac becomes largely obsolete as the liver takes over the production of blood cells, bone begins forming, and so do the kidneys, which lag behind most of the other internal organs. The heart becomes more complex as its chambers are completed. The characteristics of the heartbeat are already very much like what they will be in adult life. The embryo is now about a half-inch long.

The Seventh Week. There is marked regression of the tail. The embryo is less curled over as the back shows further straightening. The face, neck, and extremities are more clearly defined. Fingers and toes are almost always distinct at this point. The tongue takes shape, and the stomach assumes its final position. Muscles are strengthening, nerve fiber is rapidly growing, and the anus becomes evident. The cerebral hemispheres of the brain are growing large, and differentiation is occurring in the sex glands (ovaries in the female and testes in the male). The embryo is now about four-fifths of an inch long.

The Eighth Week. This marks the end of the embryonic period. The digits of the hands and feet are now well-formed, the contours of the face and body more babylike. The eyes, which have been more on the sides than on the front of the head, are rapidly converging, approaching their permanent places. Ovaries and testes are descending; a genital swelling indicates development of the scrotum in the male, while the clitoris begins to appear in the female. The lungs and heart are now in an advanced state of development. Major blood vessels are in permanent place. Taste buds and olfactory apparatus, serving the sense of smell, are present. The embryo, as it becomes the fetus, weighs about one-thirtieth of an ounce and is about an inch and a quarter long.

The Third Month

The movements of the unborn become highly pronounced in the third month. The brain and nervous system are now developed to the point where the fetus can make use of its muscles in a more coordinated manner. The fetus practices breathing, occasionally "inhaling" and then expelling amniotic fluid, making its lungs work. Its sex becomes distinct, and its kidneys begin to cope with some of the fetal waste products.

The Ninth Week. The embryo—with its odd tail and gill arches, formless face, and curled-up posture—has gradually been supplanted by the fetus. The head is now usually held up, and the body is relatively straight. Webbed hands and feet have given way to exquisitely formed fingers and toes. The face is appealing, exhibiting large eyes, button nose, and expressive lips which often as not are sucking a tiny thumb. The internal organs are in place and, for the remainder of pregnancy, mostly just need time for growth and what

54

I call "fine-tuning." Weight at this stage is about one-seventh of an ounce, and crown-rump height is about one-and-a-half inches. Teeth, fingernails, toenails, and hair follicles are all forming. The fetal heartbeat can now be detected through the mother's abdominal wall by listening through a stethoscope. The male is ahead of the female in outward sexual development, with the penis now clearly visible. The vagina and uterus are forming in the female.

The Tenth Week. The fetus is now highly responsive to touch. Eyelids close if touched; palms close into fists if something brushes across them; touched lips pucker and try to suck. Kidneys are functioning well, excreting urine into the amniotic fluid, which is constantly being recycled and thus purified through the mother's tissues. The ears, which in earlier stages of development could be seen below the eyes, are moving up alongside them. Lung and brain development are now largely complete. Bone growth is rapid. The fetus is now more than two inches long.

The Eleventh Week. Organs undergo further refinement, with emphasis on the intestinal and digestive systems. The tooth buds that will give rise to all of the baby's temporary teeth are now in place. The fetus attains two-and-a-half inches and weighs about a third of an ounce.

The Twelfth Week. By the end of this week, the fetus will be more than three inches long and weigh as much as an ounce. Its head still dominates, but the limbs are well-shaped and its rib structure is visible through the skin. The digestive system is complete. Blood is beginning to be produced in the bone marrow. The brain has taken on the overall anatomical features that will characterize it for life.

"It's Just a Blob."

I cringe whenever I hear someone utter the phrase, "It's just a blob," which the pro-abortionists frequently use to refer to the fetus in the first and even the second trimesters of development. Even some pro-abortion scientists refer to the fetus, at this and later stages, as "a mass of cells" or "mere tissue," in efforts to justify not only abortion, but even also experimentation on the unborn. Some who employ this terminology are genuinely ignorant of the facts; some others, I suspect, are willing to overlook the biological facts, convinced that abortion is an acceptable means to a desired end.

The facts, of the sort we have been reviewing, make it abundantly clear that even the early embryo is anything but a "blob," "mere tissue," or just a "mass of cells." The so-called Harvard Criteria, established by a committee at the Harvard Medical School in 1968 to define death, would, if applied to the fetus, reveal a *living* human being. The Harvard Criteria, now widely used and accepted in medical schools and hospitals, state that death is determined by four things: lack of response to external stimuli, lack of deep reflex action, lack of spontaneous movement and respiratory effort, and lack of brain activity.

There are few, if any, scientists who would dispute the fact that the fetus exhibits *none* of these "lacks" well before the conclusion of the first trimester and thus, by the Harvard Criteria, is sufficiently "alive-and-kicking" that, were it an adult, it would be treated to every effort available to *keep* it alive. Movement of the fetus has been recorded on film as early as Day 36; reflex mechanisms are definitely intact by Day 42. The embryo responds to touch in the sixth week and sometimes earlier. As fetologists come up with better means of probing the world of "inner space"—the world within the womb—they are forced to keep moving back the dates at which the embryo/fetus is found to be capable of various functions.

A flat electroencephalogram (EEG) indicates a lack of "brain waves" and brain activity in a person as a hospital seeks to determine point of death. Yet the five major areas of the adult brain are already clearly delineated in the six-week-old embryo, and EEG tracings have been detected as early as the fifth week.

Dr. Thomas Verny, psychiatrist and fetologist, has com-

mented on the application of the Harvard Criteria to the unborn as follows:

> These physiological guidelines are the best we can devise, since
> ego, spirit, self, soul—whatever name one chooses to define
> human life—lie well beyond our measurement tools. The fact
> that the unborn test 'alive' by all four criteria raises significant
> questions about our current attitudes toward abortion.[1]

I oppose *all* definitions of human life that are based on
"developmental criteria" subsequent to fertilization. Nonetheless, I welcome the honesty of researchers such as Dr.
Verny who see—and point out—the illogic of positing one
"developmental" standard of life-and-death for adults and
then quite another (far more restrictive) one for the unborn.

The brain-activity issue reemphasizes the pitfalls of trying
to use developmental criteria. Until the 1950s, it was widely
believed that the unborn exhibited *no* brain activity until birth.
Later, when researchers began doing brain-wave readings on
just-aborted fetuses, that firmly held notion had to be discarded. Even the embryonic brain has now been shown to
exhibit electrical patterns similar to those seen in adults, in
both sleeping and waking states and in other states of consciousness produced with various drugs. As early as the
mid-1960s, one well-respected researcher, Dr. Hannibal
Hamlin of Massachusetts General Hospital, was obliged to
report: "At an early prenatal stage of life, the EEG reflects a
distinctly individual pattern that soon becomes truly
personalized."

Once again, we see old "truths" fall into disrepute with
the forward march of scientific research. Once again we perceive the danger of basing life-and-death decisions on imperfect or obviously incomplete knowledge.

Abortion in the First Trimester

I have already discussed "menstrual extraction" as it is sometimes used to abort a very early embryo. Until the early

---

[1]Thomas Verny and John Kelly, *The Secret Life of the Unborn
Child* (New York: Summit Books, 1981), 196-197.

1970s, most abortions, legal or otherwise, were accomplished by "dilation and curettage"—forcing open the cervix and then scraping out the embryo or fetus with a curette, a loop-shaped steel knife. In the D & C, as it is known, the abortionist literally cuts the embryo or fetus into pieces and then extracts them from the womb using a polyp forceps. The D & C was time-consuming and dangerous, for the walls of the uterus are very soft during pregnancy. Perforations, profuse bleeding, and infections were not uncommon.

The D & C has now been largely supplanted by suction curettage, a method first used in Communist China and later introduced in Sweden before coming into wide use in the United States at about the time of the Supreme Court's 1973 decision. After the cervix is dilated, a hollow plastic tube with a sharp edge on its tip is inserted into the womb. Powerful, automated suction is applied, and the embryo or fetus is quickly torn to pieces and "vacuumed up," sucked through the transparent tube into a glass jar where a gauze "net" catches the pulverized tissue, permitting blood to seep through into another bottle below.

If the fetus is ten weeks or older, recognizable human body parts often emerge. Sometimes the fetus is too large to be sucked out of the womb completely, in which case manual cutting and scraping, as in D & C, is still necessary. Perforations and scarring of the uterine wall, though not as likely as in D & C, still occur with suction curettage. Bleeding can be heavy after the operation, and blood transfusions are occasionally required. Even in the "normal" post-procedural course of events, bleeding continues for a few days; it may last up to two weeks. Long-term adverse effects may include miscarriage, prematurity, or sterility in subsequent attempts to bear children.

I recall one young woman referred to me who had suffered two miscarriages and was desperate to have a child. Her history revealed that she had undergone a legal abortion prior to her current marriage. Suction curettage had been used to abort a fetus eleven weeks old. There had been perforation and a lot of bleeding. Scarring and stretching of the cervix during the abortion appeared to be the most likely reasons for the now-habitual miscarriages. When I suggested this, the woman became very angry, accusing me of being "irrationally" opposed to abortion, though I had made no anti-abortion statements whatsoever.

The woman chose to consult another doctor, and I did not hear from her again for some time. When I did, she was apologetic, stating that two other doctors had confirmed my diagnosis. Now she was no longer angry with me; instead she was furious because "they" had told her that abortion in the first trimester was entirely safe. "No one ever once even suggested the possibility of infertility," she complained.

In my conversations with this woman it became apparent that she was now also angry with herself. More than that, she was bedeviled by a sense of guilt—over having been "so naive and trusting," as she put it, with respect to "what they told me." Her conclusion: "I would never have had an abortion if I had known there was any risk at all that I would not be able to have children later on."

Granted, the majority of women who have early abortions *are* able to bear children later. But a significant number remain who encounter real problems. There is really no such thing as an "entirely safe" abortion, no matter when it is performed.

4

Finishing School

The Next Six Months

Though the end of the first trimester marks only the first third of pregnancy, the tissues of the unborn are largely differentiated and in place at that point. The tiny human being possesses most of the basic apparatus it will need to get through the remainder of its life. It now needs time for what already exists to grow before entering the world outside the womb. The next six months provide that time; the last two trimesters of pregnancy together constitute what I like to call a biological "finishing school."

The Second Trimester

The Fourth Month During this single month the fetus may more than quadruple its weight, going from one ounce to as many as seven ounces. By the end of the sixteenth week, it is likely to be six inches or more in length. The head is smaller now in relation to the rest of the body, though not proportionately as small as it will be at birth. Posture becomes increasingly erect with further growth of muscular and skeletal systems. Eyes are shut: The lids began to close in the

61

third month and will not reopen until the sixth or seventh month.

Whorled patterns in the skin of the palms of the hands and soles of the feet, first evident in the third month, are becoming permanent. The fetus now has the fingerprints the person will have for the rest of its life. Other whorls, of fine, downy hair, cover much of the body. This fine hair, called "lanugo," is flat against the skin, following its whorled grooves; it helps the fetus maintain proper body temperature. On the upper lip the lanugo suggests a faint mustache. There is a hint of eyebrows.

The ears of the fetus begin functioning in the fourth month. There is little doubt that the fetus hears well, gradually becoming accustomed, as pregnancy progresses, to the voices of its mother and father, its brothers and sisters. It may even become accustomed to certain voices on TV, to traffic sounds, and so on.

The lungs, though largely complete, are still collapsed. The heart is pumping several quarts of blood through the fetus each day. The brain now has many convolutions. The external female genitalia, which lag in development behind those of the male, become better developed, and the primitive egg cells have now clustered into their ovarian nests.

The Fifth Month. By the end of the twentieth week, the fetus may weigh a pound and exceed eight inches in length. Though in years past the unborn had almost no chance of surviving outside the womb at five months, that is changing. There have been isolated reports of babies surviving with birth weights in the neighborhood of a pound. Some years ago the standard medical texts declared that *all* fetuses weighing less than 1,000 grams (about 2 1/4 pounds) were doomed if born prematurely. Even infants weighing 1,500 grams were given little if any chance of survival.

As recently as a few years ago, despite much improvement in the situation, it was still generally believed that babies weighing between 750 and 1,000 grams had only a one-in-three chance of surviving. Now, at the best-equipped neonatology centers, nearly *70 percent* survive, an accomplishment many knowledgeable researchers would have called impossible only a few years ago. Little wonder that some neonatologists believe we will eventually be able to maintain babies weighing half a pound or even less outside the womb successfully.

It is in the fifth month—between the sixteenth and twentieth weeks—that the mother will often begin to feel her baby moving about in the womb, though the sensations will not yet be strong. This is the period that used to be called "quickening." There are still a few people who mistakenly believe that only at "quickening," when the movements can be detected, is the baby *really* alive.

It is intriguing that the fetus has been shown to have a very firm hand grip in its fifth month of life. Some have wondered why this should be, since it obviously doesn't need a strong grip in the womb. To me, this is symbolic of the unborn's early "firm grip on life." But, in any event, as the threshold of "viability" is thrust further and further back, things that appear to be superfluous in the womb may prove quite useful outside the womb.

A substance emerges from the skin cells and sebaceous glands in the fifth month called the *vernix caseosa.* The vernix is a somewhat waxy, cheesy substance that sticks to the lanugo and generally coats the fetus, further helping it to maintain proper body temperature while also protecting the better developed and thus now more sensitive skin from the alkaline amniotic fluid. It may also help protect against skin infections. It tends to make the amniotic waters somewhat "muddy."

By the end of this month fingernails and toenails are present and growing, and the nipples have appeared over the mammary glands of both sexes.

The Sixth Month. The fetus is much more active now. If the woman by some chance didn't "feel" her baby in the fifth month, she'll definitely feel it now. Channels of communication between the baby and its parents broaden. The father may be able to hear the fetal heartbeat by merely putting his ear to the mother's abdomen. But he should be careful; the actively "swimming" fetus may decide to flip over and stick an elbow in his father's ear. It is, in fact, often possible at this stage to identify a fetal foot, elbow, knee, or buttocks pressing up against or suddenly poking into the abdominal wall.

The observant mother may also now learn the sleeping patterns of her unborn child, for there will be periods when the baby will drift off—apparently sometimes dreaming. She may even feel the fetus stretch upon awakening. Gentle tapping on the abdominal wall may be all that is required to rouse the fetus from sleep, should the mother want reassurances that it is "still there." When occasionally the fetus hiccups, the mother will *know* it's there; by the rhythmic twitching in her stomach, the mother may think it is she and not the baby who has the hiccups.

Hair follicles and sweat glands develop. Cartilage gives way to real bone. The testes are near the scrotal sac. The eyelids reopen. At the end of the second trimester the fetus may weigh almost two pounds and finally attain a foot in length.

The Third Trimester

During the final three months of pregnancy, the fetus will more than triple its weight, tipping the scales on average at about 7 1/4 pounds at birth. It will average about twenty inches tall. As its size increases, its quarters in the womb become cramped, cutting down on the amount of movement that is possible.

The Seventh Month. The baby's weight increases to about three pounds. Hair on the head is now long enough to cut in many instances. The downy body hair has begun to recede, and the skin is becoming less wrinkled. Chances of survival outside the womb increase significantly; the fetal brain is now better equipped to control breathing, swallowing, and so on. In the presence of air, the fetus would now be capable of crying out. The eyes are open and capable of some light sensitivity.

The testes have now descended into the scrotal sac, where they will remain for life. The ovaries of the female, however, remain within the body. The difference is accounted for by the fact that sperm cells require cooler temperatures to survive than egg cells do; it is cooler in the scrotum than it is in the rest of the body.

The Eighth Month. The fetus may weigh as much as five pounds and exceed fourteen inches in crown-rump height. The skin is now smooth and pink, filled out by the fat deposits that account for most of the weight gain at this point. The fetus is rapidly getting ready for the potentially cooler environment outside the womb.

The Ninth Month. At approximately 7 1/4 pounds, the about-to-be-born baby measures about fifteen inches in the sitting position and twenty inches from head to toe. Movement in the womb is almost impossible, as the baby fills most of the available space. Normally the baby is all but standing on its head at this point, ready to pass through the birth canal and meet the world head-on.

This month is a time for final touches. The process is largely cosmetic as the newborn sheds much of its waxy protective coating, lanugo hair, and old skin cells. Fingernails and toenails are growing rapidly (and may in fact have to be clipped shortly after birth). Eyes are almost always blue at birth because pigmentation is still incomplete.

Growth in the womb has almost stopped, and the placenta begins to regress. The mother may notice an actual *decrease* in weight during the final weeks of pregnancy. It is essential, of course, that the rate of growth of the fetus slow down and halt as birth approaches; it has been calculated that if fetal weight gain continued even at the rate in evidence during the eighth month, the baby would weigh two hundred pounds by the time it was one year old—and several million tons by the time it attained its twentieth birthday!

Birth. Though undeniably a very important life event, birth does *not* mark the beginning of life. One might as well believe in voodoo as in the old notion that life begins with the cutting of the umbilical cord or the first breath of air. The baby's body is no less oxygenated inside the womb than it is outside. Its mind and spirit are no less alive within the womb than they are outside of it. Birth tells us something of the *when* of life, but not the *what* of life. It is not the event that tells us what we are.

Labor is usually said to occur in three stages. In the first stage, the cervix opens fully so that the baby can exit from the womb. In the second stage, the baby passes through the birth canal and is "born." In the third stage, the "afterbirth"—the placenta—is expelled from the womb. The total length of labor varies a great deal, but on average will last twelve to eighteen hours for a woman having her first child and six to nine hours for other mothers.

The delivery phase of labor—birth itself—technically begins when the cervix is fully dilated and the baby begins to emerge. This stage may last from a half-hour to three hours. The amniotic sac bursts, usually at the beginning of the delivery phase. "Crowning" occurs when the baby's head becomes visible, and then birth proceeds rapidly. If crowning still has not occurred after two hours of "pushing" and "bearing down" by the mother, the doctor will probably use forceps to help pull the baby from the womb. Once the baby's head has fully emerged, the rest of the baby slides out relatively easily.

The baby's head usually emerges "face down," that is, looking away from the mother. It turns to one side or another, though, as soon as it can, instinctively trying to face the mother. The head is still somewhat flexible, because not all its bones have fully fused together. This makes the "tight squeeze" through the birth canal tolerable for both mother and baby. Almost all births occur "head first." Only 3 percent are "breech" births: buttocks first.

After the baby has emerged, the doctor announces, "It's a boy!" or "It's a girl!" The baby usually starts to breathe immediately, first clearing its nose and mouth of irritating mucus, then perhaps letting out a healthy wail. Sometimes the mucus has to be removed manually with a suction device. Still wet from the fluids of the birth canal, the baby must be dried to preserve body heat. The umbilical cord is clamped and cut, and the baby is either wrapped in a blanket or placed on its mother's stomach.

The state of the baby's health is immediately assessed, with special emphasis on heart rate, respiratory effort, muscle tone, reflexes, and color. Silver nitrate is applied to the newborn's eyes. This is a precaution against eye infections caused by maternal gonorrhea, something a woman may have without knowing it; infection from this source can cause blindness. Vitamin injections are sometimes given; the baby is weighed and measured and its footprints taken as a precaution against "mix-up" of babies in the hospital.

Expulsion of the placenta usually follows birth within an hour, often beginning within five or ten minutes of delivery of the baby. The placenta detaches itself from the uterus; the uterine contractions tend to squeeze shut the placental blood vessels, reducing bleeding. Usually the placenta comes out "whole," but if parts of it stay in the uterus, they will have to be removed by the doctor. Expulsion of the placenta generally takes no more than twenty to thirty minutes and is a minor "delivery" compared with the birth of the baby.

I have now reviewed the major events of the second and third trimesters, culminating in birth itself. Remember that even from the very beginning of the second trimester, the fetus is largely complete. By the end of the twentieth week the fetus, given the present state of our technology, already has a chance—though still slim—of surviving outside its mother's womb. It can only be a matter of time until even younger fetuses will similarly be "viable" outside the womb.

Let us consider now what happens when this new life, which, by almost any standard, is "a going concern," is interrupted by abortion during the second and third trimesters of pregnancy.

Late Abortion: Its Impact on Fetus, Mother, Doctor

Abortion after the first trimester is achieved by one of four methods: dilation and evacuation (D & E); or injection into the womb of saline solution; the use of prostaglandins; or hysterotomy (surgical removal of the fetus). D & E is nothing but a somewhat more complicated D & C, as described in chapter 3. There is disagreement over the relative safety of D & E compared with other second-trimester methods of abortion, but some claim it is the safest. There is no doubt that it is significantly more dangerous than the suction method used to end earlier pregnancies. Saline, prostaglandins, and hysterotomy are favored for abortions occurring after the sixteenth week (late in the fourth month).

D & E: "A Grisly Jigsaw Puzzle"

In dilation and evacuation, the cervix is dilated, the membranes are ruptured, and the fetus and other "products of conception" are cut up inside the womb and then withdrawn with a forceps.

After the body parts are removed from the uterus, they are often laid out in their original relationship with each other—like "a grisly jigsaw puzzle," states Dr. Bernard Nathanson, who acknowledges having "presided over 60,000 deaths" via abortion. This procedure is to ensure that nothing is left behind in the womb. The fetus is quite large at this point; a jagged piece of bone left inside could easily cause perforation of the uterus. Even when great care is exercised, perforation and hemorrhaging can occur, because the doctor must dismember the fetus "blind"—that is, without being able to see what he is doing.

Recalling some of the abortions carried out in his clinic in New York, Dr. Nathanson described the finished "jigsaw puzzle" this way:

> One could see where the arms and legs had been ripped from the body and removed separately, how the spine had been snapped in two and removed with dispatch, how the skull had been crushed and the brain drained out before the bony parts were removed.[1]

[1]See *Aborting America* (New York: Pinnacle Books, 1981). Dr. Nathanson wrote this book after coming to oppose abortion; earlier, he had played an instrumental role in getting New York State abortion laws changed prior to the Supreme Court's 1973 decision.

The D & E is performed between the twelfth and eighteenth weeks in many centers, though some use the procedure through the twenty-fourth week, up to and beyond the point at which fetuses have been known to survive outside the womb. Death and dismemberment do not come in a "moment," but over a matter of minutes. Limbs may be torn off and the body lacerated well before the brain itself is crushed. Who is to say that a sixteen-to-twenty-four-week-old fetus—or even a younger one—does not experience some form of terror, some unspeakable silent pain, when its protective bag of waters is abruptly pierced by cold steel and its limbs torn, its body slashed, its spine snapped, and its head crushed?

I will no doubt be accused of "sensationalism" by some people merely for posing that question. But in fact, even some who favor the current abortion laws have conceded that by the end of the second trimester, the fetus is a feeling, responsive entity, by then attaining a "sense of self." One fetologist/psychiatrist has said that the fetus at this point is already possessed of the rudiments of "ego." Another has called the unborn at this stage "a fascinating human being."

Pro-abortionists who express any reservations at all about D & E see as its major disadvantage the fact that "physicians and nurses have more emotional reactions to it" than they do to some other methods of abortion.[2] The failure of D & E to become more popular than it is may be accounted for by the ghoulishness of the procedure which, Dr. Smith states, "many physicians find . . . extremely distasteful."[3] This failure is surprising in view of the claim by the Center for Disease Control that D & E is the safest method of abortion in the second trimester. Yet the fact that it is not as widely used as its alleged safety would suggest shows that when doctors and nurses are *required to see* what they are doing to the fetus in the process of abortion, *they are less likely to do it.*

Unfortunately, many of these same doctors will quite willingly perform other second-trimester abortions, using

[2]E. Dorsey Smith, *Abortion: Health Care Perspectives* (New York: Appleton-Century Crofts, 1982), 64.

[3]Ibid., 196.

techniques that do *not* require them to see the results of their labors. Equally unfortunate is the fact that financial return has been found to directly influence a doctor's morality when it comes to abortion. Dr. Smith, who is pro-abortion, cites various studies that indicate that "physicians are more satisfied with performing abortions when they are satisfied with their remuneration." Those whom she identifies as "liberal" in their attitudes toward abortion "perform more abortions, ask for fewer corroborating consents, charge higher fees, and more often ask for the fee in advance."[4]

"Salting Out": The Doctor Doesn't Have to See and the Mother Is Told Not to Look

The saline, or "salting out," method of abortion is most "optimally" used between the sixteenth and eighteenth weeks of gestation, though some use it through the twenty-fourth week. It was Dr. Nathanson, incidentally, who made saline the popular method it is today. He did this by introducing some refinements that speed up the procedure. It is currently the *most popular* method of second-trimester abortion in the United States, despite the fact that the Center for Disease Control and others claim D & E is safer. The saline method entails inserting a needle into the womb, right through the abdominal wall, for the dual purpose of withdrawing some of the amniotic fluid and replacing it with a highly concentrated salt solution. The saline quickly surrounds the fetus, and some of it is swallowed by the fetus. Some say this kills the unborn within minutes; however, others acknowledge that it may take an hour or more in many instances before the baby dies. The salt poisons the fetus and helps induce uterine contractions that expel the fetus from the womb some twelve to forty-eight hours after the injection. With certain drugs first used in this context by Dr. Nathanson, delivery of the—usually—dead fetus will occur within a few hours of injection.

[4]Ibid., 191.

I have inserted the word *usually* here, because there have been numerous reports of babies being born *alive* after "salting out." Most of these emerge with a horribly burned appearance, and few survive for very long. An example of one that *did* survive was reported in the *Bakersfield Californian* (September 25, 1973). A nurse, though horrified by the sight of a live baby where a dead one was expected, nonetheless valiantly fought to save the baby, which weighed four pounds. A doctor ordered her to withdraw the oxygen she was giving it, despite her protests that to do so would kill the baby. "Wasn't that the original idea?" the doctor demanded. The nurse persisted in giving the oxygen anyway, and the baby survived and was placed for adoption.

It is difficult to say precisely what pain a baby being killed by salt solution might experience. Some have likened the burned look of the fetal skin, after salting out, to the appearance of skin that has been exposed to napalm. There is no question that the salt poisons the fetus, inducing hemorrhage and shock before death.[5]

It is necessary that a woman undergoing a saline abortion remain conscious during the salt injection so that her reactions can be monitored. Emergency measures must be taken at the first sign of shock, for this may mean that the needle has pierced one of the woman's blood vessels. Introduction of the salt solution into her bloodstream can lead to rapid convulsions, cardiac failure, and death. Even when the procedure goes "smoothly," it is generally highly unpleasant for the woman. It is no doubt much worse for the fetus, which almost always begins to thrash about (I can only imagine in what agony) when the salt invades its nest. "Many women," Dr. Smith observes, "cry or express fear of pain and anxiety about feeling fetal movements during the procedure."[6]

After the salt injection, the woman returns to her bed and usually delivers a dead baby some hours later. The doctor

[5]See "Fetal Pathology and Mechanisms of Death in Saline Abortion," *American Journal of Obstetrics and Gynecology,* 120 (1974): 347–355.

[6]Smith, *Abortion: Health Care Perspectives,* 70.

most often is nowhere in evidence by this time, which helps account for the method's popularity among physicians who perform abortions. The nurse is left to deal with the fetus and the mother. Dr. Smith argues that a woman should be discouraged from looking at her dead fetus, even though she might request to see it. Women who don't want to see or who might be emotionally upset by what they see should be advised when "not to look," Smith advises, adding that, in general, the nurse who does her job best is the one who does not indulge in "overbearing sharing of information."[7]

For all the talk among pro-abortionists of the fetus being "just a blob," a "mass of cells," or something else less than human, those who engage in the business of abortion show a remarkable degree of squeamishness and—I can't help concluding—bad conscience over what they are doing.

Studies accepted by pro-abortionists (summarized in Dr. Smith's book) indicate that for every 100,000 women who have a saline abortion, 17 to 25 will die. This compares with 7 deaths per 100,000 from D & E. Some anti-abortionists say the death rate from abortion is actually much higher than reported. They claim that there is a natural inclination among those who provide the raw statistics to present the rosiest picture possible, since abortion is their business. In addition, in order to spare relatives, there is a natural tendency not to list abortion as an official cause of death. It is easier to put down something else as cause of death, such as adverse reaction to anesthesia. Whatever the true maternal death rate might be from abortion, there is little dispute over the one abortion statistic that I find the most sinister: There are 1,500,000 unborn human beings killed by abortion in the United States every year.

The Prostaglandins: Redefining Abortion

There seems little question but that extracts of prostaglandins, naturally occuring fatty acids, are considerably safer than sa-

[7]Ibid., 74–75.

line for inducing labor and expelling a fetus. Side effects, though commonplace, tend to be relatively mild (nausea, vomiting, diarrhea); most can be fairly easily counteracted. The prostaglandins act by inducing labor; unlike saline, however, they do not poison the fetus, and therein lies the rub. Though safer than saline, they are more likely to produce *live* babies. This is why many hospitals do not like prostaglandins and why they remain "experimental" even though they have been around now for many years.

Perhaps we will redefine abortion eventually or, rather, restore it to its original meaning—that of *separating* the fetus from its mother, not necessarily killing it. Prostaglandins, or other drugs modeled after them, might help toward that redefinition. If abortions are performed in late preganancy, when the fetus has a chance of surviving outside the womb, why not develop methods that have some chance of delivering *live* babies, which could be placed for adoption if the natural mothers decided they really didn't want them?

Hysterotomy: "Are we to Wring their necks?"

Hysterotomy is the name given to major surgery that is used to end a pregnancy late in the second (or even in the third) trimester. It is used when other methods have failed or when it is too late in pregnancy to employ those others. The Supreme Court has ruled that abortion is legal, under varying circumstances, right up to full-term birth, nine months after conception. What the Supreme Court failed to recognize—or admit—is the fact that *there is no method* of aborting these late-in-term fetuses.

Hysterotomy is nothing other than Caesarean section. We call it "hysterotomy" if we want to kill the baby, "Caesarean" if we want to save it. In either case, however, a live baby is likely to emerge. If it is to die, then it must die of neglect. Cases have been reported in which living babies, following failed abortion by "hysterotomy," have been disposed of while actually breathing. But there have also been numerous reports of nurses fighting to keep such babies alive. To those who continue to suggest that hysterotomy be used to achieve late abortions, Dr. Nathanson asks, are we "to take living fetuses fresh from the uterine wound and wring their necks?"

It should be noted that hysterotomies are performed not only at the "risk" of delivering live babies, but also at the risk of maternal life. The maternal mortality rate for complications of hysterotomy is about ten times that of saline abortion.

5

Medicine's Youngest Patient

Learning the physical facts that attend life's rites of passage—
from the events that precede conception to birth itself—can
engender empathy and respect for the unborn human being
more powerfully than anything else in my experience. Still,
even after full exposure to the facts, a few of my patients have
resisted the idea that the fetus is an "individual." For some,
the idea that we do not attain individual "personhood" until
we are independent of our mothers and can live outside the
womb dies hard.

Two developments, however, rarely fail to impress the
"resisters." One is the growing ability of medical science to
treat the ills of a fetus while it is still in the womb. The other
is medicine's great and continuing progress in sustaining the
fetus, at ever earlier ages, outside the mother's womb when
it becomes necessary. Increasingly the knowledge that we
have been accumulating about the unborn for decades now
is moving from the realm of academic medicine into the prov-
ince of clinical application. The inevitable consequence of this
is a heightened recognition of the unborn as a distinct, viable,
human individual worthy of our respect and compassion.

The Fetus as Patient: Diagnosing
and Treating Fetal Ills

Medicine has a new patient, its youngest ever: the fetus. Doctors are continually finding ways not only of diagnosing fetal illness, but also of treating the fetus while it is still in the womb. Whereas in the past, diagnosis of some serious illness in the womb usually meant a death sentence for the fetus—via induced abortion—now, more and more, these diagnostic tests are a prelude to salvaging babies, not destroying them.

Several years ago, David Rorvik wrote a cover story for *Look* magazine detailing the first known successful human fetal surgery ever performed.[1] Dr. Stanley Asensio of the University of Puerto Rico School of Medicine operated on a woman seven months pregnant, cutting through the abdominal and uterine walls to expose a fetal leg so small and delicate it could only be held with hands cushioned in fluid-filled gloves. A catheter was inserted into a blood vessel near the groin; most of the baby's blood, afflicted by Rh disease, was drained and replaced with fresh blood. At the end of the three-hour operation, the catheter was removed, the incision in the groin closed, the leg teased back in place, and the uterus and abdomen stitched shut.

Drugs that keep the uterus from contracting were used to prevent premature labor. A baby girl was born three weeks later via Caesarean section. The child was still anemic, but not nearly so anemic as it had been. The operation had almost certainly saved its life. This was the *ninth* time the mother had attempted to bring a child into the world alive; all her other babies had died of anemia in the womb. The baby girl delivered by Dr. Asensio survived and developed normally.

What had made prenatal diagnosis of Rh disease possible was a breakthrough pioneered by Dr. Douglas Bevis of Great Britain. In the early 1950s, Dr. Bevis, ignoring the centuries-old taboo of invading the womb, injected a long needle through the abdomen of a pregnant woman and drew out a few drops of amniotic fluid. Analysis of the bilirubin (a pig-

76   [1]"Surgery on the Unborn" (November 4, 1969).

ment of red blood cells) in the syringe enabled the enterprising doctor to tell just how sick the fetus was. Other doctors soon began using this technique—called amniocentesis—to determine when it was necessary to induce labor early so that the baby could undergo immediate blood transfusion and thus perhaps be saved. Dr. Bevis' breakthrough quickly cut the mortality rate from Rh disease in half at many hospitals.

Often, of course, it was not possible to save the baby by inducing premature labor. Some babies badly afflicted by Rh disease were too young to withstand premature birth. A further breakthrough was achieved in 1963 when Dr. A. William Liley of New Zealand accidentally pierced a fetal abdomen during amniocentesis. The fetus jumped, but seemed otherwise no worse for the experience. This emboldened Dr. Liley to begin injecting fresh blood directly into the abdomens of fetuses. In the earlier stages of pregnancy, the fetus can absorb red blood cells injected this way. This development further reduced deaths from Rh disease.

Various methods have been devised to enable doctors to guide needles through the abdominal wall and into the uterus of a pregnant woman while monitoring their progress on television screens. Ultrasound is now used to provide an image of both the fetus and the needle. A serum has been developed that has largely overwhelmed the Rh problem, but amniocentesis is in wider use than ever before. By drawing off small samples of amniotic fluid, doctors can analyze not only the fluid itself, but also cells suspended in it that have sloughed off from the fetus.

By analyzing the fluid itself, doctors can determine if the fetus is in distress from lack of oxygen, whether it needs a blood transfusion, whether it has a wide variety of metabolic problems. By analyzing the cells, doctors can detect numerous chromosomal abnormalities that may indicate a variety of defects. Since there is some risk to both mother and fetus from amniocentesis (there is a slight chance, for example, that it will trigger premature labor), it is not a routine procedure. It is usually reserved for pregnant women over age thirty-five or for those whose families or spouses have some history of genetic disease. Some of these genetic diseases do not manifest themselves in the parents but can be passed on to their children, where they may be manifested as serious defects.

Some people are carriers of sex-linked genetic diseases—disorders associated with the sex chromosomes that can only be passed on to children of one or the other sex, depending upon the specific disease. Amniocentesis can tell "at-risk" parents what their chances of bearing a defective baby will be. Even some who oppose abortion may want to know, so that they can have time to prepare themselves for the challenge of rearing a child with special needs.[2]

Fortunately amniocentesis can sometimes diagnose problems in time to do something about them—before birth. Other diagnostic tools are also coming into wider use. These include amniography and fetoscopy. The fetoscope is a small viewing device with a light source that can be inserted through the maternal abdomen for a direct look at the patient-within-a-patient. Amniography entails injecting a special dye into the amniotic fluid; this does not harm the fetus, but shows up on X-rays specially designed for this task. Since some of the dye is swallowed by the fetus, it is possible to examine even the inside of various organs to see whether obstructions or other defects exist.

Although Dr. Asensio performed his historic operation on a fetus more than a dozen years ago, others have only recently followed in his footsteps. There have been some spectacular successes. Doctors at Moffitt Hospital at the University of California in San Francisco, for example, have now successfully operated on fetuses both inside and outside the womb (removing and then replacing them after treatment). Diagnostic tests in one case revealed that a woman who was carrying twins was in danger of losing one of her babies due to a blocked urinary bladder. Using ultrasound to guide them, the San Francisco fetal surgeons inserted a tiny catheter through the mother's abdominal wall and into the amniotic sac, then—directly on target—into the distended

[2]Information on genetic screening is available by writing to the National Genetics Foundation, 9 West 57th Street, New York, NY 10019.

bladder of the distressed twin. The fluid was drained off. Both twins were healthy at birth. More recently the same team of doctors partially removed a baby from the womb, repaired a kidney defect, and then tucked the baby back into the womb from which it was born four months later.

Doctors in Denver have treated fetuses suffering from hydrocephalus, an accumulation of fluid on the brain. They implanted shunts through the skulls of the fetuses for the purposes of draining off the fluid, the accumulation of which can kill or seriously deform if it is not eliminated. And in another twin case, doctors at Mt. Sinai Hospital in New York determined via amniocentesis that one twin was normal while the other was suffering from Down's sydrome. Rather than abort both fetuses, the doctor's killed the one suffering from Down's by withdrawing part of its blood while it was still in the womb. The normal baby was born in good health twenty weeks later; the withered remains of the other were also delivered. Whereas both babies would probably have been aborted in the past, the availability of new techniques which make intrauterine operations feasible spared one of them in this case.

It is not always necessary to resort to surgery or induction of premature labor in order to save a baby whose distress has been detected in the womb. In some cases where fetal metabolic defects have been discovered, treatment has involved putting the mother on a special diet, which must be maintained up until birth. Amniocentesis at Tufts-New England Medical Center, for example, revealed that a woman was carrying a child with an inability to adequately utilize vitamin B_{12}, which is essential for a number of metabolic processes. One child conceived by this woman had already died because of this disorder; even if the disorder doesn't kill the baby in the womb, it may bring severe mental impairment. After finding out that a second child was similarly afflicted, the woman agreed to an experimental new treatment rather than undergo abortion. Part of the treatment involved giving the woman extremely high doses of vitamin B_{12} in the hope that enough of it would thus reach the baby and overcome its deficit. The treatment worked, and the baby survived, though it will always need to take extra B_{12}.

Vitamins have been used to help prevent some defects as well as treat them. In a recent study carried out in the United Kingdom, women who had previously given birth to babies with neural tube defects—and thus were known to be at high risk of producing additional babies with these disorders—were divided into two groups. One group received vitamin supplementation (especially vitamin B_6 which is active in tissues that protect the spinal cord). The other group did not. Of sixty-one women who took no supplementation, six had babies with neural tube defects; none of the forty-seven women who took the vitamins had babies with these defects. Remember, however, that vitamin supplementation, especially in high doses, is something that always requires a doctor's supervision during pregnancy.

At last count there were more than thirty different defects that can be treated in the womb. There are many more, of course, that can be detected. This represents a great improvement over the situation that existed even a few years ago. Many authorities believe that within a decade there will be as many as one hundred defects that can be treated in the womb.

Maintaining the Patient Outside the Womb

Earlier in this book I touched upon some of the remarkable progress that has been made in salvaging premature babies. Infants with birth weights that would have been considered "hopeless" not many years ago are being rescued today. We are constantly moving earlier into pregnancy the dates and weights at which babies can be maintained outside the womb. This is not to say that it is easy to do so; it certainly is not. Prematurity is very costly in terms of medical expenses, time, talent, and hospital space needed to cope with it and the trauma it inflicts on both parents and the infants themselves. Everything possible should be done to avoid prematurity— by taking care of yourself and your baby.

Nonetheless, if a baby is born prematurely there is more hope than ever that it can be saved. Even a baby only twenty-four weeks old, weighing little more than a pound, can sometimes be saved at a major medical center. Any baby that weighs under 2,500 grams (about 5 1/2 pounds) is considered premature. About 250,000 "preemies" are born in the United States each year; some 18,000 of these weigh less than 1,000 grams. At medical centers equipped with top-flight neonatal intensive care units, almost 70 percent of those preemies weighing between 750 and 1,000 grams survive; below 750 grams, about 25 percent survive. Preemie survival rates at some medical centers have more than doubled in the last twenty years.[3]

A recent University of Washington study challenges those who have been saying that extremely premature babies (weighing under 1.8 pounds) should be "permitted" to die because they are likely to be badly deformed or retarded, if they survive at all. "Because of the great increase in mortality and also the presumed extremely high morbidity of infants weighing less than 800 grams (1.8 pounds), this birth weight has been suggested by some as a reasonable and ethical cut-off," states Dr. Forrest C. Bennett of the University of Washington's neonatal intensive care unit.

Some of the babies in the UW study had, in fact, been "set aside" to die in various hospitals. The UW study gave them a reprieve—and they were moved to the neonatal unit. Some 20 percent of these "hopeless" babies survived, according to Dr. Bennett's report in the journal *Pediatrics*.[4] A decade ago *less than 2 percent* of such infants would have survived. Equally important, the survivors in the UW study did *not* suffer the serious handicaps that prevailing "medical wisdom" has been predicting. Until the results of this long-term follow-up study emerged in 1983, most doctors had been accepting as fact the oft-heard claim that nearly 50 percent of all of these very-low-weight infants (under 800 grams) would suffer very serious mental and physical handicaps.

[3]See "Before Their Time," *Science 82* (August):68-78.
[4]Reported from the *Chicago Tribune* in the *San Francisco Sunday Examiner-Chronicle* (March 7, 1983):A12.

The UW study shows that only 19 percent of these babies turned out to have handicaps—and *none* were of the disastrous nature projected.

"Our findings are very upbeat," Dr. Clifford J. Sells, one of the neonatal unit team members, has commented. "If an infant survives, the mother doesn't have to be afraid of taking a severely damaged child home. They have an excellent chance of being normal."

In the past couple of years the public has become increasingly aware that some hospitals have had a policy of "letting" babies considered "hopeless" die, usually through cessation of feeding, i.e., starvation. Attempts to stop this have been resisted by some in the medical profession, as well as by some legislators and some members of the mass media. It is clear that both doctors and laypeople need to be better educated about the facts of prenatal life. A case that made the headlines in 1983 involved a baby that was permitted to die because, the doctors claimed, it had defects that would make its life "meaningless." Some editorial writers echoed this sentiment. This particular baby *did* have problems more severe than those noted, for example, in the UW study. Nonetheless, they were not problems sufficient to justify infanticide.

Commenting on this particular case in a letter to the editor of the *San Francisco Chronicle* on May 2, 1983, Dr. Count D. Gibson, Jr., professor and chairman of the Stanford University School of Medicine, wrote:

> Your April 24 editorial, "Reagan and the Doctors," was so inaccurate and its conclusions so confused that it requires urgent clarification. Infant Doe was born with a tracheo-esophageal fistula and Down's syndrome [mongolism]. The fistula is generally correctable by a standard surgical procedure with an excellent prognosis. There was no "undoubted future of pain and suffering" implied in Infant Doe's surgical problem at all. As to a "bleak human experience," I assume you were referring to children with Down's syndrome. To understand them, you should become better acquainted with them and their relatives, who live with them and love them. Are these members of society to be deprived of ordinary medical care and dehydrated until they die? . . . They represent a completely different circumstance from that of the brain-dead pa-

tient whose life-support systems are terminated. Do you really believe that the Down's syndrome person does not lead a "meaningful life"? These are questions which, in my view, cannot be left solely to the parents and a physician.

I have long argued that the parents of preemies, as well as the hospitals, need to "turn on the intensive care." I warn the parents of preemies that their babies may not look as plump and pink and appealing as full-term babies do, but they can still respond to affection and attention and, in fact, need it even more than the full-term babies. You should not be intimidated by the sight of your baby in the incubator with multiple tubes attached to its tiny wrinkled body. Nor should you let hospital staff keep you completely away from your baby. The "more enlightened" medical centers are recognizing a baby's need to have its parents nearby, if only to stand alongside the incubator, peering in for brief periods each day. Some degree of parent-child bonding can take place even in an intensive care unit.

Some of the doctors who struggle against great odds to save premature babies are occasionally beset by some of the same ambivalence that can strike the parents of these babies. There is always the worry that after all the effort and expense the child, perhaps because it is not entirely perfect, will be unable to make a good adjustment to life. But most of these doctors continue to struggle to save these babies; indeed, they become more ingenious in their efforts every year. Sometimes they are rewarded for their efforts by parents who send them news of children about whom they all perhaps once had doubts—children who have now brought something of great value into the lives of their parents; children who, however imperfect, have found some happiness for themselves. One noted neonatologist, Dr. Philip Sunshine of Stanford University, quotes the Indian philosopher Rabindranath Tagore: "Each newborn child brings the message that God is not yet discouraged with man."

The Impact of Knowledge

Patients who know the most about what is going on in the womb are, almost invariably, the ones who take the greatest responsibility and thus show the greatest respect for the unborn lives they are nurturing. Some of my patients have undergone remarkable changes that can only be related to their degree of prenatal knowledge. One woman in her first pregnancy stubbornly ignored my advice to stop smoking, get more rest, and generally take better care of herself. She did not become a "believer" until a friend of hers, also a heavy smoker and social drinker, had a stillbirth just a month before my patient was to deliver. When it arrived, the baby was in adequate though not optimal health.

Meanwhile, frightened by what had happened to her friend, my patient had begun studying the effects that diet, smoking, drinking, and so on can have on the unborn. I helped the woman with her "education," supplying her with papers and references and showing her slides of normal and abnormal fetal development. In her next pregnancy, this woman was the model mother-to-be. The fetus had ceased to be something vague and slightly unreal; it assumed an individual indentity, a human presence. The woman behaved as I feel all pregnant women should, nurturing the unborn as if it were already in her arms. This woman—like so many others who have taken the time to study the life of the unborn—had come to realize that motherhood begins not at birth, but *at conception.*

6

The Psychological Life of the Unborn

The evidence for the existence of a complex physical life of the unborn, as documented in preceding chapters, is overwhelming. Yet some still doubt that the fetus has any sort of *psychological* identity and thus is still not fully a "person." It is argued that in any event, the fetus cannot be communicated with in a psychological sense, even if it can be communicated with physically. I regret that I myself have been guilty of this misconception in the past. Consider this confident-sounding statement:

> Neither the thoughts nor the experiences of the mother can affect the unborn child. The newborn child is the product of its genes. Since there is no nervous connection between the mother and her fetus, it would be impossible for any of her sensations to be transmitted directly to her child at any time. Up to the time of birth, the mother has scant influence on her child (aside from the condition of her own health).

This is a passage from the book *From Conception to Birth* by Roberts Rugh, Ph.D., and myself.[1] Since the writing of that book, more than a decade ago, I have changed my mind on

[1](New York: Harper & Row, 1971), 54.

this issue. Both new research and some old research that has been reevaluated make it clear that the thoughts and experiences of the mother during pregnancy *can* and *do* affect her unborn child. This is not to say that every expectant mother need worry about what effect her every thought is having on the baby—she needn't; but I am convinced that *major* maternal emotional currents *do* affect the unborn, for good or bad. No direct "nervous connection" is required in order for this to happen, as you will see.

Psychology in the Womb

The more researchers study the unborn, the more they learn of its abilities, both conscious and unconscious, to sense its environment. We know now too that *emotions* can have powerful *physical* effects on the body at every stage of life. In view of that it is not surprising to discover that an expectant mother's emotions affect not only her body, but also her unborn child's. These effects are both physical and psychological. Paternal emotions can influence the unborn, because the mother's emotions are inevitably affected by her relationship with her mate.

Over the years, doctors have been eager to reassure expectant mothers that their thoughts and emotions cannot adversely affect their unborn babies. Part of this eagerness has derived from the natural desire to reassure the mother; some of it derives from ignorance. Doctors who persist in telling women these things may be well-meaning, but in fact they may do both their patients and the offspring more harm than good. If you do not believe that how you feel about yourself and your baby during pregnancy can have any effect, then you are unlikely to try to actively communicate with your baby and make friends with it at a time when it is highly receptive and impressionable: *before* it is born. In that case an important opportunity to do yourself and your baby a great deal of good may be lost.

Studies indicate that women who bond with babies still in the womb (as well as immediately after birth) generally have offspring who are mentally and physically healthier throughout their lifetimes. Babies who receive psychological nurturing before and just after birth are also less likely than others to lead violent and criminal lives, other recent studies show. The point of this present discussion is to make clear that you will not be wasting your time and effort if you try to communicate your love and acceptance of your baby well before it is born. These studies, furthermore, provide additional evidence of "meaningful" life before birth.

I will not repeat what I have related in previous chapters with respect to the early development of the brain and nervous system. It suffices to say that nerve tissue begins forming at the very earliest stages of development. Science has already declared the fetal brain capable of things it said were not possible only a few years ago. Who knows what further capabilities future research will reveal? We know already that even embryonic nervous tissue is "open" to maternal communication via brain chemicals called "neurotransmitters." This is a finding with enormous implications: It means that the mother's emotional states can affect the unborn almost from conception onward.

Various studies have demonstrated that neurotransmitters, hormones, and other complex biochemical messengers can pass from the mother into the developing embryo or fetus. In experiments with pregnant animals that were exposed to different forms and levels of stress, it has been further demonstrated that this stress can manifest itself in disordered neurotransmitter activity within embryonic nerve cells. Even small deviations from normal neurotransmitter activity can result in significant changes in the nervous system as a whole that may affect not only physical functioning, but also such behavioral characteristics as aggression. Thus, even before the unborn is capable of conscious thought, it is susceptible to maternal emotion and, to some extent, the biochemical shaping of future behavior.

Psychiatrist Thomas Verny notes in *The Secret Life of the Unborn Child* that some researchers now believe the embryo, even in the first weeks of life, "possesses enough self-awareness to sense rejection and enough will to act on it."[2] These same researchers think this might help account for a number of "unexplained" spontaneous abortions in women who seem to be in excellent health. Dr. Verny points out that this is still theory; but the idea is not really so preposterous when we think of "self-awareness" at this stage in terms of the sort of biochemical sensitivity I have mentioned. It is not inconceivable that thoughts—conscious or unconscious—can lead to spontaneous abortion very early in pregnancy. Such "thoughts," however, would have to proceed from very deep-seated and powerful fear of or hostility toward pregnancy, completely overriding the more natural nurturing instincts of an expectant mother.

Dr. Gerhard Rottmann of the University of Salzburg in Austria has conducted a complex study of pregnant women and then followed the progress of their offspring.[3] He found that women whose declarations that they truly wanted their babies were confirmed by psychological testing (showing that this was true at the unconscious as well as the conscious level) had the least troublesome pregnancies and birth experiences and had the healthiest children, both mentally and physically.

On the other hand, women who claimed they wanted their babies, but really didn't (as revealed by psychological testing and evaluation), had children who tended to suffer from both physical and behavioral disorders. Interestingly, there were also a number of women who said they *didn't* want their babies—claiming, for example, that children would interfere with their careers—but in whom testing revealed a hidden desire for offspring. A significant number of these babies, confused by the crossed signals they received in the womb, also exhibited behavioral disturbances.

The general conclusion from studies such as these has been that the most important factor in determining the well-being of the newborn is maternal attitude during pregnancy. If a woman really wants the baby she is carrying, she can

[2](New York: Summit, 1981). 19.
[3]See *Geist und Psyche,* ed. Hans Graber (Munich: Kindler Verlag, 1974).

often suffer even extreme stress and still give birth to a healthy child. A study carried out by Dr. Dennis Stott has shown that the strong, persistent emotional stress that touches the woman directly, causing her to have doubts about the wisdom of having a child, is most likely to result in the birth of a behaviorally disturbed or physically unhealthy baby.[4] Almost every woman will encounter some stress during pregnancy; it is not the occasional "blow up" or fright that endangers the child, but rather, the *unrelenting* kind of pressures and stresses for which the woman can find no solution that does the real damage. The most common source of this kind of stress, Dr. Stott reported, is on-going marital strife, some problem between husband and wife that goes unresolved throughout pregnancy. In a subsequent study, Dr. Stott declared an unhappy marriage relationship one of the unborn baby's biggest perils.[5] Indeed, on the basis of his findings he estimated that children born of such unions have more than 200 percent greater than normal risk of emerging from the womb with significant physical or psychological damage.

Most important, then, is the woman's attitude toward her baby: If she accepts and rejoices in her pregnancy, she and her unborn child can withstand all manner of stress. Next in importance is marital harmony: Even before the baby can hear in the womb or think consciously, it is capable of sensing discord between its parents. If its mother is in constant turmoil, its own environment will be tainted by the biochemistry of fear and hostility, grief and anger. Ideally one's differences with one's mate should be settled well in advance of any pregnancy, but failing that, every effort should be made to solve problems as early in pregnancy as possible. There's more at stake than just your feelings or those of your mate.

It is evident that there are numerous ways in which com-

[4]"Follow-up Study From Birth of the Effects of Prenatal Stresses," *Developmental Medicine and Child Neurology*, 15 (1973): 770-787.
[5]Reported in "Children in the Womb: The Effects of Stress," *New Society* (May 19, 1977):329-331.

munication can take place between the unborn and its mother. The language mother and child share may be strictly bio-chemical early in pregnancy, but it is a well-developed language nonetheless. Later in pregnancy, especially from the fifth or sixth month onward, the unborn is increasingly capable of *directly* sensing its environment. By this time, Dr. Verny believes, its ego is functioning. It is developing a sense of self and is more and more capable of detecting and differentiating various emotions. Part of this ability comes from the advancing development of ordinary sensory apparatus.

The fetus at twenty-four weeks, for example, can hear what is being said outside the womb. It does not have to understand the words to sense what is being communicated; pitch, tone, and volume of voice often suffice. If the fetus hears its parents' voices raised in anger, it will become agitated, often kicking and thrashing in its confined space. But it can and will also respond to soothing tones, to the reassuring voices of its parents, to the "feel" of their hands stroking it through the mother's abdominal wall.

But there is more to it than this. A number of researchers believe there are "sympathetic," intuitive pathways of communication between mother and child. These "channels" may be open throughout pregnancy. Though this kind of communication cannot yet be fully explained in ways that satisfy scientific methodology, its existence is at least suggested by a number of observations. Some babies who come through pregnancy without major physical difficulty nevertheless seem to have somehow sensed their mother's rejection of them in the womb, leaving them psychologically troubled.

Dr. Verny relates a story told to him by Dr. Peter Fedor-Freybergh, a well-known professor of obstetrics and gynecology at the University of Uppsala in Sweden.[6] A baby delivered by Dr. Fedor-Freybergh appeared to be very healthy at birth; but when placed at its mothers breast, it turned its head away—something that babies that bond with their mothers never do. After similar attempts to get the baby to breast-feed failed, Dr. Fedor-Freybergh decided on an im-

[6]*The Secret Life of the Unborn Child,* 77–78.

promptu experiment. He asked another nursing mother if the baby could be placed at her breast, to see what would happen.

What happened was that the baby immediately began nursing! And thereafter it continued to reject its own mother's breast. Upon close questioning, the baby's mother finally admitted that she had never wanted the baby—a fact she had concealed from everybody, she said, because she knew her husband badly wanted a child. This revelation came as a shock to all concerned—except the baby, who, as Dr. Verny concludes, had apparently known it all along. Bonding could not take place immediately after birth because it had failed to occur earlier, in the womb. The mother was willing to "fake it," but the baby wasn't.

Psychological Impact of the Birth Experience

Bonding—that special mother-child attachment—begins well before birth. Even so, the events occurring right after birth are an important continuation of the process. To help provide the best environment for the completion of this process, I have recommended that couples embrace a method of birthing that is as gentle and natural as possible, avoiding or reducing anesthetics and analgesics. It is important that both mother and baby be as alert as possible so that their awareness of one another can be at its peak during this critical postbirth period. Drs. Marshall Klaus and John Kennell of Case Western Reserve University's department of pediatrics are among those who first documented the far-reaching importance of bonding immediately after birth.[7] Others have since confirmed their findings and have found that a good bonding experience immediately after birth results not only in better children, but also in better mothers—mothers far less likely than others to abuse their children.

Other investigators have discovered that humans have

[7]"Maternal Attachment: Importance of the First Post-Partum Days," *New England Journal of Medicine,* 286 (March 2, 1972): 460–463.

a remarkable ability to retain memories of their birth experiences, though often only at the unconscious level. The way in which we are born and the things that happen to us immediately after birth can have enormous impact on us throughout our lives. Dr. David Cheek, a San Francisco obstetrician and leading hypnotherapist, has been particularly active in uncovering the effects of birth and our ability to retain that primal experience. He has found that many patients under hypnosis can recall a number of the particulars of their births, including the way in which they emerged from the womb, complications of delivery, and so on. In several instances Dr. Cheek was able to confirm that these recollections were correct by consulting delivery notes, some of which were decades old.

As a result of his findings, Dr. Cheek was among the first to call for a complete revamping of the way newborn babies are handled in hospitals. David Rorvik interviewed Dr. Cheek in 1973. By then, he was already recommending that

> the baby be immediately given to the mother and put to her breast the minute it is born. . . . The baby needs to feel very close to the mother right away. And this business of having the father wait down the hall is a terrible insult to the baby. I've had a number of patients burst into tears upon reliving their birth experiences and finding father nowhere in sight. The baby has heard father's voice for a long time—at least six weeks through the mother's abdomen—and if he's not there during the birth the baby may sense some rejection. When the husband does enter the picture he should speak directly to his baby as well as to his wife.[8]

A two-year investigation by the California Commission on Crime Control and Violence Prevention concluded in 1982 with the finding that "a positive birth experience—one that is gentle, loving and nontraumatic—increases the likelihood of healthy child development" and diminishes the likelihood

[8]David Rorvik, "The Fine Art of Being Put Not Exactly to Sleep," *Medical Dimensions* (January 1974):18–21.

of involvement in crime and violence later on in life. One of the experts testifying before the commission was neuropsychologist James Prescott. His studies have shown that infants who receive abundant attention beginning right after birth are far less likely than others to become violent or criminally inclined. The kind of attention he recommends is hugging, kissing, touching. "Pleasure and violence," he observes, "have a reciprocal relationship. . . . One inhibits the other."[9]

Dr. Verny discusses in his book the lasting trauma that can occur as a result of our mechanized birthing techniques, utilizing drugs, fetal monitors, forceps, induced labor, and Caesarean section. He relates the case histories of numerous individuals whose psychological problems later in life can be retraced to birth trauma. "Many children in the western world," he concludes, "continue to be born in a setting that might be appropriate for a computer, but that is wildly inappropriate for the birth of a human being."

What we must do, I am convinced, is reeducate everyone to the fact that parenting should begin *before* the child is born. A minute of prenatal nurturing is worth a month of "disciplining" after birth. Millions of words are being written and millions of dollars spent every year in an effort to understand and deal with infant psychology, childhood learning disabilities, juvenile delinquency, adolescent suicide, and so on. Costly and generally futile efforts are being continually launched to reshape the antisocial and criminal behavior of an ever-increasing number of juveniles and adults alike. Yet little or no attention has been directed toward the one period in life when behavioral disorders can be most effectively prevented: the period from conception to birth.

If we make friends with our children before they are born, we will have a friendlier world, and all it will cost us is a little time and a little love.

[9]See "Hugging Prevents Brain Damage," *Omni* (November 1982):48.

Part 2

The Debate: Life or Death?

Not, I'll not, carrion comfort, Despair, not feast on thee;
Not untwist—slack they may be—these last strands of man
In me or, most weary, cry *I can no more*. I can;
Can something, hope, wish day come, not choose not to be.
                    —*From "Carrion Comfort"*
                    Gerard Manley Hopkins

7

The Debate: An Overview

What the Court Said

The abortion debate today focuses primarily upon the law, as interpreted by the United States Supreme Court, which makes it legal for women to have abortions under most circumstances through the sixth month of pregnancy. The debate is about something else, as well, however—something far more significant. It is about a newly emerging ethic which may dramatically change society for all time. I will attempt here to put the debate into its proper perspective and then define my own position with respect to the issues that are raised.

On January 22, 1973, the U.S. Supreme Court handed down its historic seven-to-two decision (*Roe v. Wade*) making abortion legal throughout the land. The dramatic result of that ruling is evident in the current abortion statistics: 1.5 million legal abortions are now performed in the United States each year. Under the 1973 ruling, the individual states were forbidden to prohibit abortions performed for any reason during the first trimester of pregnancy, that is, during the first three months. The decision to abort was to be left entirely to the "woman and her physician." During the second trimester, the Court declared, the states could intervene only to set standards for abortion clinics and the doctors who performed the abortions. The Court made it clear, however, that it did not mean to limit access to abortion by this stipulation.

The Court sought to at least partially justify its decision on a concept of "viability," which it defined as the point at which the fetus is "potentially able to live outside the mother's womb, albeit with artificial aid." The time of "viability," the Court added, "is usually placed at about seven months (twenty-eight weeks) but may occur earlier, even at twenty-four weeks."

Abortion, the Court further ruled, *could* be performed after "viability"—that is after the second trimester—unless the states specifically "proscribed" it—that is, prohibited it. Even in the presence of such a proscription, however, a woman could still have an abortion in the third trimester if a physician declared that her "life or health" were endangered by pregnancy. The exact wording of the ruling on this point is as follows:

> If the State is interested in protecting fetal life after viability, it may go as far as to proscribe abortion during that period, except when it is necessary to preserve the life or health of the mother.

In summary, the Court ruled that prior to "viability," the fetus is not worthy of the protection of the Constitution; between "viability" and birth it is worthy of that protection, but only under some circumstances and only if the states so decree.

Since 1973 the Court has made a number of other decisions related to abortion. In 1976 it ruled that neither husbands or parents could interfere with their wives' or daughters' decisions to have abortions. In 1979 it ruled even more specifically that unmarried, minor females are permitted to have abortions without parental consent. That same year, in a separate ruling, it declared that the definition of "viability" would thereafter be left to the physician; lower courts and legislatures were forbidden to make laws or rulings establishing "viability."

In 1983, the Court struck down an Akron, Ohio, ordinance that had required that abortions after the first trimester of pregnancy be performed in hospitals; that women seeking abortions be given information about the possible medical complications of abortion and about the developmental status of their unborn babies and be told of alternatives to abortion; that unmarried females under age fifteen obtain parental or court consent prior to aborting; that there be a twenty-four-hour "cooling-off" period between request for abortion and actual abortion; that aborted fetuses be disposed of in a "humane and sanitary manner." The Court's ruling was highly significant, because the Akron ordinance had served as a model for similar requirements in some fifteen states.

In general, legislation by the states and rulings by lower courts seeking to limit access to abortion or push back the age of "viability" have been struck down by the Supreme Court and some of the federal courts. Those who seek to overturn the 1973 decision have focused recently on proposed legislation that would define protectable human life as beginning at the time of conception. This legislation, sponsored by Jesse Helms of North Carolina, was tabled and in effect killed by a vote of 47 to 46 in the U.S. Senate in late 1982. The same or similar legislation and a proposed constitutional amendment that would give Congress and the states "the concurrent power to restrict and prohibit abortions" are likely to be reintroduced, perhaps in somewhat different form, in future sessions of Congress.

Sociology Versus Biology

More important, though, than what has happened since abortion was legalized in 1973 is the question: What moral and social factors made possible that ruling? How had society come to justify legal abortion?

One thing is certain: The Court's 1973 decision was *not* based on scientific findings that the "unborn" is not alive or is not human. In fact, the Court dismissed that concern in these words:

> We need not resolve the difficult question of when life begins. When those trained in the respective disciplines of medicine, philosophy and theology are unable to arrive at any consensus, the judiciary, at this point in the development of man's knowledge, is not in a position to speculate as to the answer.

The Court ruled that the non-"viable" fetus is not a "person" and is thus ineligible for protection under the Fourteenth Amendment to the Constitution, which declares that no government "shall deprive any person of life . . . without due process of law."

The Court rested its case heavily upon sociological rather than biological concerns. It justified its conviction that a woman has an almost absolute right to control her own body, even when she is pregnant, upon a concept of "right to privacy." It was also influenced by its perception of the social costs of "unwanted" children, the economic and emotional plight of unwed mothers, the horrors of illegal abortion, and so on. The decision, in my view, was a dramatic expression of the newly emerging "quality of life" ethic that places the "greatest good for the greatest number" over the welfare and sanctity of the individual. But in addition, there were some specific events, trends, and developments that almost certainly helped to bring the new ethic into focus with respect to the abortion issue.

Until the 1960s there was little medical or social support for abortion except in the rare instances when the mother's life was clearly jeopardized by pregnancy. In the sixties, however, a number of factors converged to gradually weaken resistance to abortion. Society, especially urban society, was entering into a period of convulsive unrest triggered by rapid technological changes, which in turn stimulated sometimes unrealistic social and economic expectations; by a war that bitterly divided generations and ultimately the country itself, "radicalizing" large segments of the population in the process; by racial strife and rapidly increasing crime and violence. The 1960s saw an ever-increasing number of women entering the work force and, like many other minority groups, demanding political and economic equality.

In the midst of all this came the latest and most significant part of the so-called sexual revolution. This revolution was fueled not only by women seeking equality with men, but by medical technology—specifically, the development and wide dissemination of the birth-control pill. Here at last was something that gave large numbers of people, especially women, the hope that they might be able to exert some considerable control over their reproductive destinies. This feeling was given further encouragement by other dramatic advances in genetic and reproductive medicine, advances that suggested that man would soon be able to control not only his own reproductive schedule, but perhaps even his evolutionary future.

In a word increasingly beset by social and economic problems and bedeviled by a subtle element of male guilt, abortion began to loom more attractive than it ever had before. (When the sexual revolution occasionally "failed," that is when a pregnancy occurred despite the precautionary Pill, it was the woman who had to go to some back-alley "butcher" or bear a child she didn't want.) Not only would legal, socially sanctioned abortion relieve men of some of their guilt and women of some of their burdens, it would also, or so it was argued, give society some "cost-effective" solutions to problems of overpopulation, welfare, juvenile delinquency, and so on.

The 1962 thalidomide tragedy awakened the world to the ever present possibility of serious birth defects.[1] Rapid medical progress in diagnosing such defects before birth gave further impetus to abortion; it was seen as the most decisive means of "preventing" such defects. And with women finally bold enough to speak out on rape and incest, both of which sometimes resulted in pregnancy, further socially acceptable

---

[1]Thalidomide was a sedative and anti-emetic drug in use in Europe for several years prior to 1962. When used in early pregnancy, it resulted in severe malformations and defects in fetuses. It is estimated that between 2,000 and 3,000 babies with deformities attributable to thalidomide were born in West Germany between 1959 and early 1962, and another 500 such babies in Great Britain.

101

"indications" for abortion were discerned by growing segments of the population.

By the late 1960s some states had already begun reviewing their restrictive abortion laws; a few passed more "liberal" laws at that time, though all still required that each case be reviewed by a panel of physicians. New York was the first to break rank: In 1970 the state passed legislation that provided for virtual abortion-on-demand through the twenty-fourth week of pregnancy. The time was right to test laws in states where abortion was prohibited entirely. It was the challenge of the Texas law by a woman who used the pseudonym "Jane Roe" that eventually reached the Supreme Court, with such far-reaching results, in 1973.

The New Ethic

Underlying all these events was the evolution of nothing less than a new ethic. This was recognized, with explicit reference to the abortion issue, as early as 1970 in an editorial in *California Medicine,* which was then the official journal of the California Medical Association.[2] The editorial acknowledged that abortion—which the editorial did not oppose—is the "taking of human life." The movement toward legalized abortion, it said, was dramatic evidence of the gradual demise of an essentially Christian ethic that had long illuminated medical practice in the Western world and, in fact, Western society as a whole. This was an ethic, it said, that for centuries had zealously upheld "the intrinsic worth and equal value of every human life, regardless of its stage or condition." In place of the old ethic, the one which holds sacred *each* human life, the editorial added, there was emerging a utilitarian "quality of life" ethic—one that purports to seek the greatest good for the greatest number, even if that means that some individuals must suffer or die in the public interest.

Justice Harry Blackmun, in penning the majority opinion for the Supreme Court in *Roe v. Wade,* recognized, if only

[2]"New Ethic for Medicine and Society" (September 1970).

obliquely, this shift in morality when he objected to the Hippocratic Oath of medical ethics by which we doctors had been guided for centuries. The oath specifically forbids abortion. Justice Blackmun objected on grounds that the oath discriminates in favor of the Christian viewpoint while leaving the pagan world unrepresented.

It should not be assumed, of course, that simply because medical establishments and high courts have declared that a new ethic is abroad in the land, it is, perforce, the preeminent ethic. The tide, however, does seem to me to favor the new ethic, at least at this point in human history. Still, battle lines are being drawn, and there are people in all walks of life—Christians as well as non-Christians, liberals as well as conservatives—who are assiduously resisting the new ethic, convinced that it will ultimately undermine the freedom of *all* of us, not just the freedom of the unborn or others too weak to fight for their natural rights. The debate, therefore, is not simply over whether abortion should be sanctioned, but also over whether the ethic that is increasingly being used to justify it is wise and moral. Those who believe that it is neither urge a revival of and renewed commitment to the ethic that holds each human life to be sacred and worthy of the protection of the law.

The Position of the Author

I oppose abortion. I do so, first, because I accept what is biologically manifest—that human life commences at the time of conception—and, second, because I believe it is wrong to take innocent human life under any circumstances. My position is scientific, pragmatic, and humanitarian. My definition of man, for the purposes of this book, is purely biological. Biological man is the product of the forty-six chromosomes that combine to confer a unique identity at the time an egg is fertilized by a sperm. I am not qualified to address issues of soul and spirit in any detail. It is my assumption, based entirely on faith, not science, that to the extent that biological man is imbued with a soul, he acquires that property at the moment of conception.

103

I reject all the arguments which seek to justify abortion on grounds that the unborn is not a living being or is somehow less than human, mere "potential life," or part of a "continuum of life that has neither beginning nor end." I resist and reject the new ethic which—even when it recognizes that the unborn child is not only human life, but meaningful human life—still considers that life expendable under many circumstances. The pragmatism that this ethic purports to embrace is, in my view, illusory; an ethic that makes any class of individuals expendable "in the interests of society" ultimately imperils that entire society.

I have always opposed abortion, except in those cases where the life of the woman is genuinely endangered by a continuation of the pregnancy. For some time, however, my position was one of "passive resistance." It was not until the 1973 Supreme Court decision that I made a public statement opposed to abortion, as the foreword to this book explains.

It comes as a surprise to some of my associates that I oppose abortion, particularly since I pioneered some of the technology that made the so-called test-tube babies a reality. Because some of those who have opposed abortion have also opposed the creation of human life in the laboratory, the assumption has often been made that I would automatically be *pro-abortion*. Thus, I've learned a good deal about stereotyping. Now that I've made my anti-abortion views known, some seem to think that, "in order to be consistent," I will also become Catholic, vote for "hard-line conservatives," oppose civil rights, birth control, and education, and adopt some anti-feminist views. At the very least some seem to expect me to account for my new outspokenness by declaring that I "saw the light" as a result of a mystical religious experience. After all, I am told, "Everyone knows that abortion is a religious issue."

In truth, there are some—a very few, in my experience—on the pro-abortion side who would like to see me embrace this stereotype. But I refuse to become wedded to either a conservative or a liberal political and ideological stereotype.

Far from being inconsistent with "liberal" or "humanist" principles, I believe that abhorrence for abortion squares precisely with those values. I believe that the clearest-headed pragmatists and "situational ethicists" *must* oppose abortion if they truly do prize the "greatest good for the greatest number." The Golden Rule is pragmatism of the highest order.

As for my position on abortion in my own medical practice, I try not to preach or proselytize. If a couple comes to me seeking an abortion or advice on abortion, I am pleased to be able to present my viewpoint. But for the most part, my approach is to show rather than tell. I show the woman or the couple pictures of the unborn at various stages of development, explain what we know about the fetus at critical stages, and then let the parent or parents make up their own minds. If presenting the facts in an objective manner makes me guilty of attempting to "bias" the decision, then I stand guilty as charged.

In a subsequent chapter I will provide some case histories related to various components of the abortion issue. We do well to remember that behind the barrage of words that make up the raging debate, there are real people, real feelings, real hopes, fears, triumphs, and tragedies.

8

Life Begins At:

(A) Conception? (B) Implantation? (C) "Viability"?
(D) Birth? (E) Graduation From Princeton? (F) Never?

The Question in Perspective

Those who ask when life begins and think they have thus
arrived at the core issue of the abortion debate are mistaken.
The United States Supreme Court said that it could not answer this question, but it nevertheless proceeded to make
abortion legal. Many others who favor abortion have been
even more forthright in dismissing the question as essentially
irrelevant insofar as their position is concerned. Some in the
vanguard of the pro-abortion movement have acknowledged
that the fetus *is* human life and that abortion *does* take that
life. Some have even been willing to concede that the life
thus taken is "meaningful." Yet they have still advocated
abortion because, they argue, its social benefits outweigh its
costs to society. At the real core of the debate, then, is—once
again—the clash between an ethic that makes the sanctity of
human life an absolute and a new ethic that renders that life
relative and sometimes expendable.

The "Viability" Issue

Some pro-abortionists regret that the Court—despite having
said that the issue of when life begins could not be resolved   **107**

and would not thus figure in its decision—went on to predicate its ruling, at least in part, on the concept of "viability." Those who have chosen to acknowledge that abortion is the taking of human life (albeit the taking of life for reasons they argue are justifiable) wish that the Court had done the same— that, in short, it had ruled that legal abortion is in the best interests of society and let it go at that. By introducing the biologically shaky concept of "viability," the Court seemed to betray some doubt about the validity of its assertion that the question of when life begins need not concern it. If the question mattered at all—and the Court's reliance upon the concept of "viability" suggests that it did—wasn't the Court obligated to err on the side of caution, that is, on the side of possible life? Shouldn't it have accorded to the unborn—which might prove "viable" at any time, given the on-going advances of medical science—the benefit of the doubt in the form of a presumption of life?

The Court said "viability" was "usually placed at about seven months (twenty-eight weeks) but may occur earlier, even at twenty-four weeks." No one is sure how the Court decided on those dates. Even the legal briefs introduced by the attorneys who were seeking to overturn the Texas law and thus legalize abortion cited a 1971 medical text that said "viability" *could* occur as early as the twentieth week. Dr. Bernard Nathanson believes the Court simply followed the lead of New York State. The New York law, passed in 1970, set twenty-four weeks as the point of "viability." It is instructive to learn how that date was arrived at.

In his book, *Aborting America,* Dr. Nathanson relates this story:

> I had the opportunity to ask Assemblywoman Constance Cook about how the architects of the bill had arrived at the twenty-four-week limit. She told me, a little apologetically, that doctors regarded the twentieth week as that point at which the expulsion is no longer an abortion but a premature delivery, and the fetus is an "infant" born alive, or a "stillbirth" if born dead. The older English common law figured viability, the point at which a prematurely delivered fetus had a reasonable chance to survive, at twenty-eight weeks. At this point

in her exegesis she paused a beat or two, then said: "We split the difference." And that, children, is how laws are written.[1]

This is clearly a matter worth making a point of, for if "viability" has any validity whatever in determining when human life begins or should be protected, then it needs to be very clearly defined. It is a matter of life-and-death.

The Court could not have chosen a weaker concept than "viability" on which to rest any part of its case for the beginning of protectable human life. The whole concept is highly relative and constantly changing. Besides the fact that even as the Court issued its decision there were babies alive and well that had been delivered earlier than twenty-four weeks, there was also the medical certainty that babies would be found "viable" at ever younger ages as medical science advanced.

An abortion law truly based on "viability" would require constant redefinition. What was not considered protectable human life last year might be this year. If we were to take the Court at its word, we would find ourselves with a law that makes last year's "abortions" this year's "homicides" in some cases. I have maintained human embryos in "laboratory wombs" for several days; some mammalian fetuses have been "grown" in laboratory cultures all the way to the stage at which they develop beating hearts. It appears inevitable that the day will come when the unborn will *always* be potentially viable outside the womb. What happens to the abortion law then?

Some may argue that the Court redeemed itself in January 1979, when, in the course of its decision outlawing Pennsylvania's abortion-control bill, it declared that the physician would henceforth be entrusted to determine "viability" in each case. "Viability" was redefined as occuring when the physician decided there was "a reasonable likelihood of the fetus' sustained survival outside the womb, with or without artificial support." The recognition that "viability" is a constantly changing concept is, of course, welcomed. Correct reasoning, however, does not always lead to correct conclu-

[1]Page 69.

sions. The impact of the 1979 decision has been, as three dissenting Justices made clear in their sharp retort to the majority, to further diminish the protection of the unborn. The 1979 decision took away from the states the opportunity, granted under the 1973 decision, to protect the fetus when it is "potentially able to live" outside the womb and declared that henceforth only a physician could make this determination. Since the physician making the decision is almost certain to be one who has a vested interest in performing abortions, we seriously doubt that many women will be turned down in their requests for abortion on grounds that their babies are "viable."

The Question of When Life Begins

When the Court declared in 1973 that experts in "medicine, philosophy, and theology" do not all agree as to when human life begins, it was telling the truth, of course. On the other hand, something that is true can still be highly misleading in a particular context. Experts in medicine, philosophy, and theology rarely if ever agree on anything. To use a generalization of this sort to brush aside a very important issue is, in my view, unjustified. Beyond that, I feel compelled to point out that the judiciary has traditionally relied upon science and medicine, not philosophy or theology, to help it separate the living from the nonliving. Scientific findings are accepted as "fact" in courts of law. Religious and philosophical declarations, even if regarded as fact by millions of people, are accorded in the courts the lesser stature of "opinion." To begin with, then, I believe that the Court should have focused on medical science, wherein disagreement exists but not to the extent implied by the Court.

It should be understood that in making its assertion about disagreement on this matter, the Court did not conduct a survey of scientists, theologians, and philosophers. It did not call before it even the world's leading reproductive biologists. Its job is to review cases already heard by lower courts, not to explore new ground. It was aware, however, that there were many different ideas about when life begins. Over the years some had said it began with "quickening"—when the mother first felt the baby stir in the womb. Others said at birth. Those ideas had been discredited, and there were few in science who any longer accepted them. There were theologians, philosophers, and mystics of many persuasions who had radically different ideas about life and its beginnings. Some said no one could be sure when life began because no one was sure when the soul or spirit, whatever its description, entered the body or came into being. As I have pointed out, however, it seems doubtful that the Court would let concepts of soul or spirit influence its interpretation of secular law.

But the Court knew that there were some differences even among scientists. Some said life begins at conception. Others said at implantation, when the embryo attaches itself to the lining of its mother's womb. And then there were some scientists who said that no one could determine life's biological beginnings because it is a "continuum, *collectively* without beginning or end." It is up to society, some of these scientists said, to decide when *meaningful* human life begins. Therefore, they did not directly deny the existence of *individual,* biological life from the moment of conception onward, but argued that until such time as the life acquired certain capabilities, it need not be considered worthy of society's respect.

The only concrete scientific evidence placed before the Court attested to the biological facts of conception and prenatal development, facts related earlier in this book. These facts supported the argument that life begins at conception or, failing that, a few days later at implantation. No scientific data were presented to refute this evidence. Despite this, the Court—using as its excuse the argument that no one could agree on life's beginnings—swept the biological issues aside and focused instead on what it clearly perceived to be of paramount importance: the sociological issues. I have no doubt that the Court was sincere in its conviction that women—and society as a whole—would be best served by legal abortion.

It takes a hard heart, indeed, not to feel compassion for

a young girl who is pregnant and unwed or for a married woman who, out of ignorance of birth control or because of poverty, has had one unplanned child after another and thus finally turns to abortion. We all recoil in horror at stories of girls and women who have become pregnant as a result of rape or incest. We are equally appalled when we hear of mercenary back-alley abortionists who maim and kill women who seek out illegal abortions. The Supreme Court justices are no less human than the rest of us; the compassion they felt for women cannot but have played a significant role in their decision. Despite this and despite my own feelings of compassion, I cannot refrain from pointing out what I regard to be serious flaws in the 1973 ruling. Nor can I extinguish the compassion I feel for the unborn, who suffer the ultimate loss in abortion.

Conception as the Beginning of Individual, Biological Life

I must emphasize again that when I talk about "human life" or about "man," I speak of biological man. When I limit the discussion to this concept, I feel confident that life's beginnings can be precisely ascertained. Moreover, when this limit is strictly imposed, there really is not as much disagreement as the Court decision suggested in 1973 or as some pro-abortionists imply today.

It has become expedient for some who once said unequivocally that life begins with conception to assume a certain vagueness on this matter now in order to accommodate abortion. Even Planned Parenthood, prior to assuming a pro-abortion stance, stated that human life begins at conception. The late Alan Guttmacher, long the leader of Planned Parenthood and a man whom I admired a good deal, in 1947 called the fertilized egg "the new baby which is created at this exact moment." In 1961, Dr. Guttmacher wrote that "fertilization, then, has taken place; a baby has been conceived." In the early 1960s, Planned Parenthood literature warned women about the dangers of abortion and explicitly stated that abortion "kills the life of a baby." No knowledge has emerged since the sixties that would cause Planned Parenthood to alter its view on scientific grounds, though alter its view it has. Indeed, all the new knowledge we have about the unborn only *further* supports the idea that here is meaningful human life. The biological facts have not changed direction. But society has.

When the Executive Board of the American College of Obstetricians and Gynecologists in 1981 issued a statement opposing restrictions on abortion, it also fell back on the argument that no one can tell when human life begins. It focused instead on what it called the "cost-effectiveness" of abortion in dealing with a number of medical and sociological problems. A number of members of the College, including me, expressed distress over this statement, which so clearly reflects the new ethic I have been discussing. Dr. Richard V. Jaynes, for example, declared in *Ob. Gyn. News:* "To say that the beginning of human life cannot be determined scientifically is . . . utterly ridiculous."[2]

The U.S. Senate Judiciary Subcommittee held hearings in 1981 on the issue of when life begins. Pro-abortionists, though invited to do so, failed to produce even a single expert witness who would specifically testify that life begins at any point other than conception or implantation. One witness said no one can tell when life begins. And in later hearings, some other witnesses took the position that human life is part of a continuum, without discrete beginning or end.

Typical of the overwhelming majority of those who testified was Dr. Jerome LeJeune, professor of genetics at the University of Descartes in Paris. "When does life begin?" he asked. "I will try to give the most precise answer to that question actually available to science. . . . Life has a very long history, but each individual has a very neat beginning, the moment of its conception. . . . To accept the fact that after fertilization has taken place a new human being has come into being is no longer a matter of taste or opinion. The human nature of the human being, conception to old age, is not a metaphysical contention, it is plain experimental evidence."

[2]September 15, 1981.

Dr. Watson A. Bowes, Jr., of the University of Colorado Medical School testified that "the beginning of a single human life is from a biological point of view a simple and straightforward matter—the beginning is conception. This straightforward biological fact should not be distorted to serve sociological, political or economic goals."

Dr. Alfred Bongiovanni of the University of Pennsylvania Medical School noted that the standard medical texts have long taught that human life begins at conception. He added: "I am no more prepared to say that these early stages represent an incomplete human being than I would be to say that the child prior to the dramatic effects of puberty . . . is not a human being. This is human life at every stage albeit incomplete until late adolescence."

Dr. Micheline Matthews-Roth, research associate of Harvard University Medical School, testified: "It is incorrect to say that biological data cannot be decisive. . . . It is scientifically correct to say that an individual human life begins at conception. . . . Our laws, one function of which is to help preserve the lives of our people, should be based on accurate scientific data."

Professor Hymie Gordon, chairman of the Department of Medical Genetics at the Mayo Clinic, stated: "By all the criteria of modern molecular biology, life is present from the moment of conception."

Dr. McCarthy De Mere, who is a practicing physician as well as a law professor at the University of Tennessee, testified: "The exact moment of the beginning [of] personhood and of the human body is at the moment of conception."

Those who argue that human life is a continuum, without definable beginning or end, often posit a "developmental" definition of what they call "personhood." In this they claim that we should become "protectable" human beings or "persons" only when we reach certain stages of development, when we become "recognizably human" or when we first evoke the "empathy" of others, or when we first develop "a sense of self." By many of the developmental criteria—some of which are more than a bit mystical—we probably would not attain "personhood" until well after birth. Another difficulty is that these criteria are often dangerously subjective and vulnerable to constant redefinition. We might, as someone perhaps only half in jest suggested, finally end up not attaining "meaningful," "protectable" life until we "graduate from Princeton." Or at least until we had passed puberty and thus completed our biological development. With so many different points to choose from, we would think that even the developmentalists would choose conception—the one developmental event without which none of us would ever enjoy a heartbeat, a brain wave, empathy, a sense of self, puberty, *or* graduation from Princeton.

Something must also be said about "implantation," the process of the fertilized egg's attaching itself to the lining of the uterus several days after conception. There are those who insist *this* is the logical point at which to say life begins; without implantation, they argue, the new life cannot be nourished and cannot survive. Though it would be convenient (for reasons I will explain when I discuss birth control in a later chapter) if life did not begin until implantation, the arguments in favor of the idea fail to sway me. Implantation is an important event, but it in no way defines life. It simply defines a condition by which life is *maintained* once it has already started.

Some others have argued that life cannot be said to begin at conception because a fertilized egg can still split, a short time later, to give rise to identical twins. I fail to be moved by this argument either. To say that it is all right to take life because it is still at a stage when it might in rare instances give rise to an identical copy of itself (i.e., to *more* life) is illogical.

Those Who Concede the Point But Advocate Abortion Anyway

As indicated earlier, there are some pro-abortionists who do not bother to dispute what I regard to be fact: that human life begins at conception. Some concede, moreover, that the life that is taken in an abortion is a "meaningful" one. It is here that the debate assumes its real identity, focusing not on whether life is being taken, but rather, on whether it is justifiable to take life for sociological reasons. Here one directly confronts the new ethic.

In the preceding chapter I cited an editorial in *California Medicine* in which this new ethic was given unusually clear and honest expression. The editorial admitted that until the new, utilitarian, "quality-of-life" ethic was firmly established, it would prove necessary "to separate the idea of abortion from the idea of killing." It pointed out "an avoidance of the scientific fact, which everyone really knows, that human life begins at conception and is continuous whether intra- or extra-uterine until death. The very considerable semantic gymnastics which are required to rationalize abortion as anything but taking a human life would be ludicrous if they were not put forth under socially impeccable auspices." But even acknowledging all that, this official journal of the California Medical Association did not oppose abortion; nor did it oppose the new ethic which, it said, might eventually extend to legal infanticide and other killings if these were perceived as improving the quality of life for the greatest number.

Dr. Magda Denes, author of *In Necessity and Sorrow: Life and Death in an Abortion Hospital*,[3] was quoted by the Chicago *Daily News*[4] as saying, "There wasn't a doctor who at one time or another in the questioning [carried out in the course of researching her book] did not say, 'This is murder.'" Dr. Denes herself calls abortion "killing," yet continues to advocate it as "necessary" for social reasons.

Dr. Nathanson has written of the ambivalence and guilt and occasionally outright-bad conscience suffered by some of his one-time fellow abortionists. Dr. William Rashbaum, an abortionist who was chief of family planning services at Beth Israel Medical Center and a faculty member at the Albert Einstein College of Medicine, told the *New York Times* that abortion is "destruction of life." He also said that for a time he was beset by images of the fetus resisting his attempts to abort it, holding on in the womb for dear life. Yet he concluded that he had no right to tell women that abortion is

[3](New York: Basic Books, 1976).
[4]October 22, 1976.

wrong, nor to deny them abortions. "I don't get paid for my feelings. I get paid for my skills."[5]

An editorial in the *New Republic* belittled most of the arguments of the pro-abortionists, asserting that these arguments almost always avoid the real issue: "There clearly is no logical or moral distinction between a fetus and young baby; free availability of abortion cannot be reasonably distinguished from euthanasia [killing after birth]."[6] But the editorial concluded. "We are for it." Though human enough, it was argued, the fetus simply is not worth the "social cost" of defending it against the "mother's will."

Mary Anne Warren, a bioethicist at San Francisco State University, also dismisses most of the pro-abortion arguments as specious. She holds that the fetus is clearly a human being. But, in her opinion, it is not a human being worthy of protection. She puts forward the sort of "developmental" arguments we have dealt with already: The fetus has to "feel pain," be "conscious" and capable of "self-motivated" activity, and so on before she is willing to protect it. The problem with such arguments is that we are still profoundly ignorant of much that transpires in the womb. The more we learn however, the more complex we discover the fetus to be; we keep setting back the dates at which the unborn is found to have various capabilities.

Warren is willing even to sanction the killing of an eight-or-nine-month-old fetus, proclaiming that the unborn even at that age is "considerably less personlike than is the average mature mammal, indeed the average fish." Even at this stage the fetus, in her view, has no more right to life than "a newborn guppy." Consequently she also sees nothing wrong with killing the unborn in order to make use of its tissues and organs in experimentation and transplantation. Infanticide is all right, too, in her view, if the baby is defective or there is no one who wants it.[7]

[5]Bernard Nathanson, *New York Times Magazine* (April 17, 1977).

[6]July 2, 1977.

[7]Mary Anne Warren, "On the Moral and Legal Status of Abortion," in *Ethical Issues in Modern Medicine,* ed. R. Hunt and J. Arras (Palo Alto, Calif.: Mayfield Publishing Co., 1977).

117

Warren's is not an isolated view. Michael Tooley of Stanford University has expressed similar ideas, maintaining that "personhood" should be withheld for a week after birth, during which time the baby could legally be killed if it fails to measure up to society's standards.[8]

The Social "Justifications" for Abortion

"The right of women to abort," Dr. Nathanson has written, "derives from a political locus, alpha's [the unborn's] right to exist derives from the very bone of a culture's morality. The 'right' to abort is not a right as that term is commonly understood, but only a 'claim.' . . . If abortion is not justified as a 'right,' then it must be justified on pragmatic grounds. . . ."[9]

The fact that those who support abortion nearly always feel compelled to try to justify their position by enumerating its social and pragmatic "benefits" seems to belie their concomitant claim that the unborn is not human or, in any event, is not worthy of protection. If that claim were true, no social or "pragmatic" justifications for abortion would be required. But setting aside that contradiction, let us examine a number of the "justifications" that have been proposed for abortion. Does abortion really offer society important benefits? In summarizing each of the claims we will first state the pro-abortion position and then analyze it.

- *"Most abortions are necessary to protect the life of the woman or to terminate a pregnancy that is the result of rape or incest or that would result in the birth of a defective child."* In more than forty years of obstetrical and gynecological practice, I have seen only "a handful" of cases where abortion was needed to save a woman's life. Pregnancies that are the

---

[8]Michael Tooley, "Abortion and Infanticide," in *The Rights and Wrongs of Abortion,* ed. Marshall Cohen et al. (Princeton, N.J.: Princeton Univ. Press, 1974).

118   [9]*Aborting America,* 256-257.

result of rape or incest are statistically rare. Abortions performed to prevent the birth of mentally or physically handicapped children are also few in number. Most abortions are not performed for medical reasons; most are elective.

When a pregnancy results from rape or incest, I believe that a rational and compassionate society should offer the victim encouragement—physical, psychological, and financial—to carry the baby to term. If the mother wishes to give the child up for adoption at birth, that can readily be arranged. Abortion does nothing to right the grievous wrong of rape or incest; indeed, it only compounds it, adding to the assault of one innocent person the taking of the life of another innocent person.

Nor can I accept the argument that abortion is justified if there is a possibility or even a high probability that a child will be born "defective," even seriously defective. My reasons for resisting this argument are both humane and "practical": Once we permit the notion that defects cancel one's humanity, we risk losing *all* real humanity and open the way for arbitrary definitions of "humanity" based upon subjective, shifting ideas of what is "normal" or "acceptable" at any given time. I am convinced that a rational society *must*—not only out of human compassion or religious conviction, but also out of pragmatic self-interest—protect even the weakest and the most imperfect of its members if it is to survive with any semblance of its freedom intact. If the defects of a child are such that the parents cannot cope with its needs, then they should be given assistance or the opportunity to place the child in a special-care environment.

I find unconvincing the oft-heard argument that a "defective" should be aborted "for its own good." What is usually meant in such circumstances is, "It will be better for *us.*" Who is to say what is good for another person? History is full of examples of geniuses who not only overcame but were *spurred* by serious imperfections and handicaps. As Francis Bacon put it, "Prosperity is not without many fears and distastes; and adversity is not without comforts and hopes." Dr. C. Everett Koop, the noted pediatric surgeon who is currently the Surgeon General of the United States, expessed the same viewpoint in an address before the American Academy of Pediatrics in 1976:

> It has been my constant experience, that disability and unhappiness do not necessarily go together. Some of the most unhappy children whom I have known have all of their physical and mental faculties, and on the other hand some of the happiest youngsters have borne burdens which I myself would find very difficult to bear. Our obligation in such circumstances is to find alternatives for the problems our patients face. I don't consider death an acceptable alternative. . . . Who knows what happiness is for another person?

Whenever people tell me that a "defective" is "better off" dead I politely suggest that they tell this face to face, if they dare, to ten *seriously* handicapped persons. If they survive the responses and still aren't convinced, I suggest they look at a number of studies on the subject, such as one published in the *Proceedings of the American Psychological Association Meeting 1971*. In this report, several Wayne State University researchers stated: "Though it may be both common and fashionable to believe that the malformed enjoys life less than normal, this appears to lack both empirical and theoretical support."

Something more needs to be said on this subject, something that suggests those who are imperfect make a special contribution to society. John Ruskin, the British essayist and critic, put it this way: "All things are literally better, lovelier, and more beloved for the imperfections which have been divinely appointed, that the law of human life may be Effort, and the law of human judgment, Mercy."

The late Jean Rostand, famed French biologist and philosopher, expressed something similar in his book *Humanly Possible:*

> I have the weakness to believe that it is an honor for a society to desire the expensive luxury of sustaining life for its useless, incompetent and incurably ill members. I would almost measure society's degree of civilization by the amount of effort and vigilance it imposes on itself out of pure respect for life. It is noble to struggle unrelentingly to save someone's

life as if he were dear to us, when obviously he has no value and is not even loved by anyone.[10]

I would disagree with Rostand only in my conviction that this is not a luxury, but a necessity in a society that would remain free.

* *"Every child should be a **wanted** child. Those who oppose abortion promote child abuse and child neglect which lead to juvenile delinquency."* It would be nice, of course, if everyone were wanted, but is one's degree of *wantedness* a logical or ethical standard by which to determine one's right to be at all? If so, then we shall have to conclude that life and death are matters henceforth to be determined in popularity contests. Beyond that, even if one accepted the central fallacy of this argument, one's wantedness is subject to change. Many children who are unwanted at some point during pregnancy end up thoroughly wanted at birth or at some later date. And some terribly wanted babies no doubt end up utterly unwanted later on.

Claims that restrictive abortion laws promote child abuse and child neglect have never been documented. If readily available abortion is supposed to alleviate these problems, there is no evidence that this has occurred. The incidences of child abuse and juvenile delinquency have continued to escalate each year.

The claim has also been made that women are more likely to commit suicide in a society that has restrictive abortion laws. Again, if this were true, the rate of increase in suicides among women should have declined after 1973. It did not. And the rate of suicide among pregnant women has remained substantially lower than among women in general.

Finally, it must also be pointed out that for many years there has been an acute shortage of newborn infants available for adoption. Hundreds of thousands of adoptive parents

[10]*Humanly Possible: A Biologist's Notes on the Future of Mankind,* trans. Lowell Blair (New York: Saturday Review Press, 1973).

are on waiting lists, competing for the few babies who become available. There are agencies ready to help girls and women through pregnancies that might otherwise end in abortion. These agencies offer psychological and financial support; they will help a woman keep her baby if she decides she wants it, or they will help arrange for adoption.

• *"A woman has a right to control her own body. The decision to abort should be left to the woman."* This claim is part and parcel of an ethic which I believe is ultimately *antifeminist:* It places on the woman the full burden of a responsibility that should, by the dictates of both biology and decency, be shared by the male. It seems to me that men have finessed women into a neat little corner where they rejoice over their "right" to impair one of their own biological functions, take the life of the unborn, and possibly do themselves injury in the process.

The feminist, of course, argues that now she has a *choice,* but does she really? The typical woman who goes to an abortion clinic is not given the information she needs to make a truly *informed* choice. It is in the clinic's financial interest to get on with the abortion. Most abortion counselors haven't the time, the background, or the inclination to tell women what abortion really entails; it is considered "counter-productive" and "bad form" even to allude to any aspect of what really happens to the unborn in the course of abortion. To show the woman pictures of the grisly process would be considered "insane"; even to show the woman what her unborn child looks like in the healthy state, with readily available slides, is also considered "beside the point."

Certainly, in the atmosphere of the abortion clinic the woman is not encouraged to look into organizations that would help her have her baby or place it for adoption. There is no room for trying to make a woman feel good about the idea of having a baby. Nor is there usually any talk of what abortion might mean to the woman in the future; the data that strongly suggest that abortion, especially in first pregnancies, may result in significant difficulty in carrying a baby to term later on is most likely never mentioned at all. "Counseling," as even some pro-abortion sources have acknowledged, too often amounts to simply deciding *when* the abortion will take place.

But beyond that, does a woman really have "a right to her own body"? I admit that the phrase has a nice ring to it and, expressed this way, it immediately makes anyone who takes exception to it appear anti-woman. (Of course, it is sometimes acknowledged that the doctor should also have a word in this, but, in truth, the doctor is generally as absent as the male in any real decision-making.) The woman, then, is encouraged to believe that she should have exclusive control over her body—a peculiar notion, it seems to me, since our laws rarely let people do with their bodies what they will.

It disturbs me deeply that the male is not encouraged by society to participate actively in the abortion decision. As things stand now, it is as if he, like the life he helped to create, did not exist. Granted, he may be relieved to find himself "invisible" in this ghastly business, but then again he may not. Not *all* men are eager to cop out; not *all* are able to. There is some evidence that men are gradually taking a more responsible role in abortion, setting up counseling centers of their own or joining together in groups to discuss their feelings about what the women in their lives haved chosen to do.

Eleanor Smith, writing in *California Living* magazine, concluded that "contrary to popular opinion, most men experience a wide range of emotions when their partners find themselves pregnant unexpectedly and opt for abortion."[11] The data presented in this and other articles indicate that women do themselves violence by excluding the male, who often ends up feeling frustrated and angry, in part because he is denied the opportunity to take greater responsibility for helping to see to it that future abortions are not "necessary."

Dr. Arthur B. Shostak of Drexel University in Philadelphia conducted a study of men whose babies were aborted. He found that for a significant number of them, the abortion experience was "more frustrating, trying and emotionally costly than public and academic neglect of this subject would

[11]"Counseling Men About Abortion" (January 17, 1982).

suggest." Many of these men, the researcher found, felt a strong sense of loss and resented the fact that they were excluded from counseling and, especially, from receiving the birth-control information that might help avoid future abortions.

One final point on this issue: Dr. Bernard Nathanson has observed that "nineteenth-century feminists were universally opposed to abortion, even after antisepsis had made it a safer procedure. They considered it yet another outrage that had been inflicted upon women by men who forced them to have abortions." He adds, "As a 'women's issue,' abortion works against the pro-choicers in that virtually every U.S. poll over the past decade has shown that women are significantly more anti-abortion than men are."[12]

- *"Abortion is a 'cost-effective' means of solving the problems of poverty and overpopulation."* Even if this claim had been documented—and it has not—I would still reject it. If taking lives is to be our "solution" for social problems, then we must surely be at the end of our social, spiritual, philosophical, economic, and scientific resources. An extremely liberal abortion law has now been on the books for more than a decade. There is no evidence that this law has alleviated any of our economic difficulties.

- *"Without abortion, overpopulation will become unmanageable."* Killing, whether of the unborn or any other group, simply cannot be accepted as a humane means of controlling population growth. And, in any event, this argument cannot be used in the United States, or many other parts of the world, where the birth rate began declining well before abortion was legalized and has continued to decline. Overlooking temporary "up-ticks" in birth rate, such as that following World War II, the overall trend in the U.S. has been downward since the early nineteenth century. The average number of offspring per family has steadily declined from 6

[12]*Aborting America,* 193.

in 1850 to 1.8 today, lower than is necessary to maintain the population at its present level.

If abortion and The Pill have not been responsible for this downward trend, what has? We do well to ask. Before we spend millions or even billions, as some have suggested, on massive programs of abortion, birth control, and sterilization, especially in Third World countries, we should make every effort to understand the dynamics of population growth and decline. This is a question John D. Rockefeller III asked himself. After much investigation, he said,

> After forty years of advocacy of family planning as a primary approach to world population, I have now changed my mind. The evidence has been mounting, particularly in the past decade, to indicate that family planning is not enough. . . . It recognizes that motivation for family planning is best stimulated by hope that living conditions and opportunities in general will improve.[13]

Psychology seems to be the most important factor. While serving as director general of the Food and Agricultural Organization of the United Nations, A. H. Boerma spoke of evidence that "there is a proportionately larger falling birthrate in areas touched by the Green Revolution, compared to those untouched by it. If indeed higher agricultural productivity does directly encourage lower fertility, then FAO's main contribution to population policy may well be to push its efforts in agricultural development at an even more rapid pace than at present." Better to spend those billions on programs like this than on setting up abortion centers.

The U.S. Agency for International Development reported a few years ago that in seventy-two of the eighty-two countries that keep reliable statistics, birth rates are declining. These include many Third World countries. Declines in some industrialized countries are now so great that they are actually causing governmental concern. The U.S. Census Bureau's top expert on Soviet demographic affairs reported in 1982, for example, that the birth rate in Russia has fallen so low

---

[13]United Nations Conference on Population, Bucharest, 1976.   **125**

that the government there has launched a "pro-natalist" propaganda drive, offering couples incentives to have children, rather than practice birth control or have abortions. The fear is that the country will suffer serious military and industrial manpower shortages by the end of this decade.

Meanwhile in the United States, demographers almost uniformly agree that population rates will continue to decline. In fact, says sociologist-demographer Joseph McFalls of Temple University, this country may also eventually have to offer incentives to encourage reproduction, just as Russia and some European countries already do. If the incentives don't work, he predicts, the government may finally have to *make its own babies* through programs of artificial insemination, surrogate mothers, and test-tube fertilization:

> Although this sounds like science fiction, it's really not so unusual for one institution, such as the family, to give up some of its functions to another, such as government. Families used to be responsible for the education of children and the care of the aged. The government does both now.[14]

• *"Abortion is safer than childbirth."* This is a broad generalization that can be dangerously misleading to the girl or woman considering abortion. Maternal mortality may be greater in pregnancy and childbirth than in abortion when we compare *all* pregnancies with *all* abortions. But the individual woman is not *all* women; the individual should be made aware that some abortions (later in term) can be more dangerous than letting the pregnancy go to term. In addition, the generalization overlooks a number of factors the individual should know about; the complications that can attend abortion, even assuming they are fewer in number than those attending full-term pregnancy, may prove *qualitatively* more severe in some significant particulars. At the very least, the assertion that "abortion is safer" needs detailed qualification.

Many abortion advocates have ignored or sought to discount reports on the adverse "side effects" of abortion. Nonetheless, there is increasing recognition of some risks, particularly in abortions involving women or girls in their first pregnancies. For example, researchers at Charles University in Prague, Czechoslovakia reported on women who had been aborted over a thirteen-year period, all of them in a hospital setting with the best gynecological care available (the equal of that found in the U.S.). All of the women, moreover, aborted during the first twelve weeks of pregnancy, when abortion is considered safest. The researchers noted serious complications, especially among "primagravidas," women pregnant for the first time. The Czechs noted a dramatically increased incidence of ectopic (tubal) pregnancies (which can be life-threatening), sterility, and miscarriages when these women later attempted to bear children. "A high incidence of cervical incompetence resultant from abortion has raised the incidence of spontaneous abortions [miscarriage] to 30-40 percent."[15]

Other studies have confirmed various aspects of the Czech study. (See, for example, *British Medical Journal* 1:1303-4 [1976]:21). For that matter, even Planned Parenthood as early as 1963, well before it immersed itself in the abortion business under new leadership, warned women in one of its pamphlets: "Abortion kills the life of a baby. . . . It is dangerous to your life and health. It may make you sterile so that when you want a child you cannot have it." The sterility evidence was scant then, but has since grown considerably.

The Czechs and others have also reported on an increased number of premature births in women who have previously aborted. A report in the *Journal of Obstetrics and Gynecology British Commonwealth* (80:418-22 [1973]) noted a *doubled* incidence of prematurity among women who had aborted. This tendency toward miscarriage and prematurity is most likely the result of damage done to the cervix when it is forced open to provide access to the fetus during abortion with the result that the taut muscle is sometimes irreversibly stretched and

[15]A. Kodasek, "Artificial Termination of Pregnancy in Czechoslovakia," *International Journal of Gynecology and Obstetrics,* vol. 9, no. 3 (1971).

torn. The increased chance of tubal pregnancy after abortion is attributed to uterine scarring (when the baby is scraped from the womb) which sometimes makes it difficult or impossible for the egg to pass from the fallopian tube into the uterus, with the result that the fertilized egg nests inside the tube itself.

Dr. Leslie Iffy, in a letter to *Ob.Gyn. News,* stated that overseas data on abortion-caused prematurity "has been confirmed recently by data obtained in the United States."[16] The effects of abortion in this respect, he added, have been particularly severe in adolescent girls who aborted during first pregnancies. Mindful of the fact that a significant number of premature babies suffer severe physical and mental defects that are costly to society, Dr. Iffy questioned the "cost-effectiveness" of abortion. Observing that pro–abortion sources estimate that some 400,000 adolescent pregnancies are ended through elective abortion annually in the U.S., Dr. Iffy calculated that this sets the stage *each year* "for an extra 25,000 premature babies . . . a substantial proportion of whom require partial or total support throughout their lives."

• *"If abortion is restricted or made illegal, women will again resort to dangerous 'back-alley' abortions."* In *Aborting America,* Dr. Nathanson calls this "a fundamental argument; one that moved us deeply in the late '60s, and one that could justify . . . abortion even if no other argument stood up." Dr. Nathanson and others who were agitating for legalized abortion at that time often spoke of as many as 10,000 women dying every year because of abortions performed by incompetent and unscrupulous operators. "I confess," Dr. Nathanson wrote years later, after he had changed his mind about abortion, "that I knew the figures were totally false, and I suppose the others did too. . . . The overriding concern was to get the laws eliminated. . . ."[17]

In truth, the number of deaths that resulted from illegal abortions was probably closer to 500 per year, he now ac-

[16]"Long-Term Costs of Abortion" (September 15, 1981):6.
[17]*Aborting America,* 196–197.

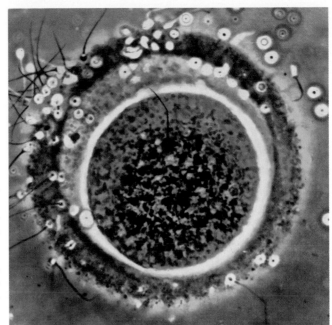

A human sperm cell penetrating a human egg (at roughly the twelve o'clock position). Thousands of sperm will eventually attach themselves to the egg's outer perimeter, but only one gains admission into its nucleus. The merger of sperm and egg chromosomes marks the beginning of a new life. (Ch. 1)

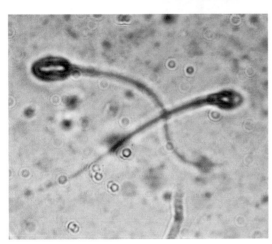

Living human sperm. The sperm with the larger, more elongate head contains the X chromosome and would produce a girl if united with an egg cell. The sperm with the smaller, oval-shaped head contains the Y chromosome and would give rise to a boy. (Ch. 1)

The human egg as it appears just after it emerges from the ovary. Cloaked in thousands of protective "nurse" cells, it looks like the moon behind a cluster of cumulus clouds. (Ch. 1)

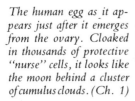

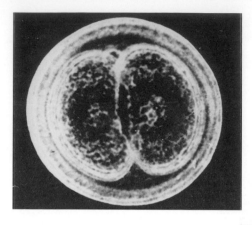

Human life thirty hours old. Here the fertilized egg cell undergoes its first cleavage, approaching the two-cell stage. Billions of cells will ultimately arise from one fertilized egg in a remarkably short span of time. (Ch. 1)

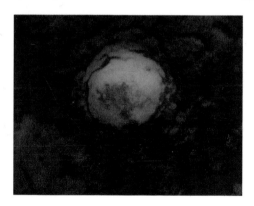

The early human "blastocyst," four days after fertilization. In this stage the new life attaches itself to the lining of the womb. Implantation will not begin for another two or three days. (Ch. 2)

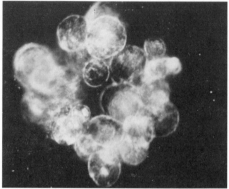

An egg implanted firmly in the uterine lining, some twelve days after fertilization. It will stay attached here for the duration of pregnancy. (Ch. 2)

The month-old human embryo. Though not yet cuddly-looking, it possesses the rudiments of most of its major organs. Its heart is already pumping blood. In one month a single cell has multiplied to millions of cells, which have organized themselves into complex structures by a process that still mystifies researchers. (Ch. 2)

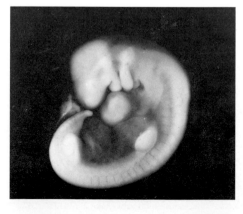

Human fetus at two months. The amniotic sac, umbilicus, and placenta are all visible. (Ch. 3)

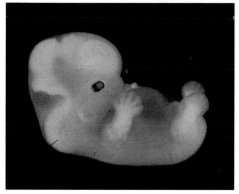

Side view of human embryo at thirty-seven days. (Ch. 3)

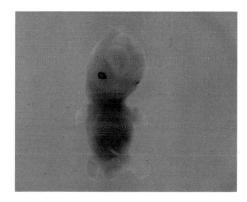

Front view of human embryo at thirty-seven days. (Ch. 3)

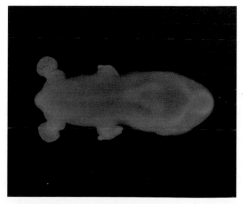

Rear view of human embryo at thirty-seven days. (Ch. 3)

Human fraternal twins at eleven weeks. Each has its own umbilical cord and placenta. (Ch. 3)

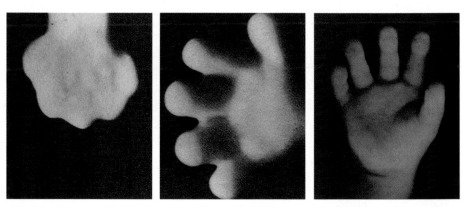

Hand development. The hand progresses from a paddlelike structure in the fifth week to "webbed" fingers in the sixth week to distinct thumb and fingers in the seventh or eighth week. The feet develop similarly. (Ch. 3)

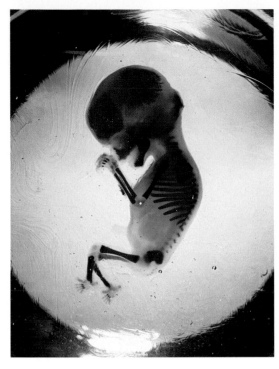

Skeletal development at three months. (Ch. 3)

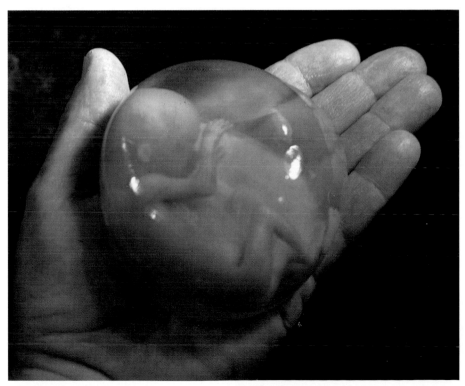

The size of a twelve-week-old human fetus relative to an adult's hand. (Ch. 3)

Abortion by suction curettage at ten weeks. (Ch. 3)

An attempt to "reassemble" the baby after an abortion has been performed by dilation and evacuation. The procedure has the purpose of ensuring that nothing has been left behind. (Ch. 4)

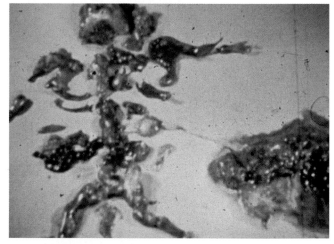

A salt-poisoned baby at nineteen weeks. (Ch. 4)

Photos on this page used by permission from Abortion, How It Is, *Hayes Publishing Co., Cincinnati.*

A sixteen-week-old human fetus sucking its thumb. (Ch. 4)

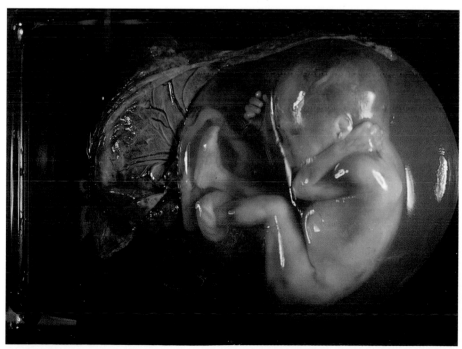

Human fetus at twenty weeks. The chorionic sac has been opened here to reveal the fetus in its "bag of waters" along with the placenta. (Ch. 4)

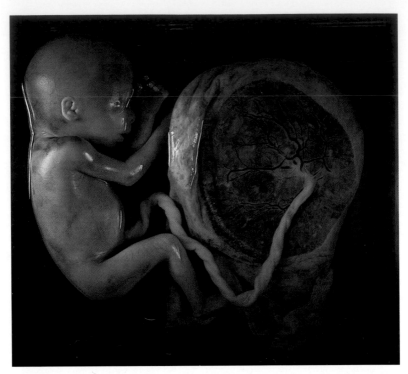

Fetus, placenta, and umbilicus in the eighth month. (Ch. 4)

Full frontal view of human fetus at twenty-four weeks. (Ch. 4)

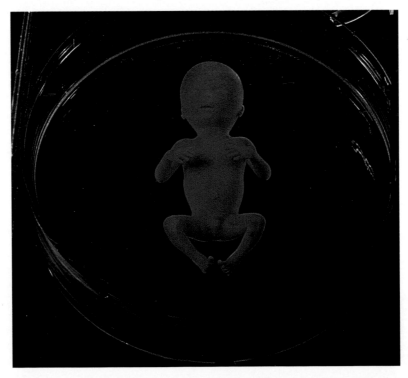

All photos, except as noted, by Dr. Landrum B. Shettles.

knowledges, adding that if abortion were to be outlawed again today there would be no return to the old days of the "coathanger" abortion. "The practice of abortion," he states, "was revolutionized at virtually the same moment that the laws were revolutionized, through the widespread introduction of suction curettage in 1970." Even a trained non-physician, Dr. Nathanson believes, can operate a suction curette "with remarkable safety."

It is instructive to note what happened when the so-called Hyde Amendment on abortion was passed by Congress in late 1977. This law related to the funding of abortions under Medicaid; it prohibited the use of such funds for abortions that were not "medically certified," i.e., shown to be *genuinely* necessary to preserve the life or the health of the expectant mother. (Abortion for rape and incest were also permitted.) Upon passage of this law there were dire warnings from the pro-abortionists that poor women, denied legal abortions, would now seek out "butchers" willing to do illegal abortions and that this would result in many deaths. Even the Center for Disease Control, a government agency, predicted that there would be as many as ninety needless deaths per year.

Follow-up study, however, has proved these predictions false. There has been no evidence of any increase in abortion-related deaths whatsoever, as even the CDC has now conceded. With the stricter requirements of the Hyde Amendment, under which there had to be some genuine medical reason for aborting, the number of authorized abortions under Medicaid decreased more than *99 percent,* dropping from 250,000 in 1977 to less than 1,500 the next year. So much for the "necessity" of most abortions!

• *"Abortion is the will of the majority and therefore should not be questioned."* Though the trend may be toward a "numbers morality," our laws for the most part are still not formulated entirely on a show of hands. When they are, even the most heinous acts would have to be accounted "right" or "moral" if a majority supported them.

Aside from that, however, is it true that a "majority"   **129** favors abortion? Polls on such complex issues are notoriously unreliable, since the way in which questions are worded or posed has enormous effect on how they are answered. Even so, however, a survey of the Gallup polls on abortion over nearly fifteen years shows that the "majority" normally opposes abortion-on-demand. When questions explicitly include abortion after the first trimester, there is even less support for abortion.

A poll of women published by *Life* magazine in November 1981 (conducted by the polling firm of Yankelovich, Skelly and White) contained wording which, in my view, encouraged pro-abortion answers by focusing on rape, incest, and genetic defects, for example, while ignoring questions that would have highlighted the *elective* nature of most abortions. Nonetheless, 56 percent of those polled said they believe abortion is "morally wrong" even though they might choose to have one under some circumstances. And 78 percent answered "yes" to the question, "Should a girl who is under 18 years of age have to notify her parents before she can have an abortion?" Another question: "If an unmarried high school girl becomes pregnant, do you think her mother should suggest to her that she have the baby or have an abortion?" "Have the baby," responded 44 percent. Only 20 percent said, "Have an abortion." The rest were "not sure." And 53 percent said federal and state funds *should not* be used to pay for abortions for women under Medicaid, with 38 percent taking the opposing viewpoint.

In an address before a Canadian gathering in 1981, Dr. Nathanson recalled the pro-abortion movement's misuse of polls and statistics to help pave the way for the 1973 Supreme Court decision:

> We fed the public a line of deceit, dishonesty, a fabrication of statistics and figures. We succeeded because the time was right and the news media cooperated. We sensationalized the effects of illegal abortions and fabricated polls which indicated that 85 percent of the public favored unrestricted abortion, when we knew it was only 5 percent. We unashamedly lied, and yet our statements were quoted as though they had been written in law.

This is a remarkable confession by any standard, coming as it does from one of the co-founders of the National Association for Repeal of Abortion Laws (probably the most important force in the drive that led to our present abortion laws) and the one-time Director of the Center for Reproductive and Sexual Health when it was the largest abortion center in the world.

Life Is Its Own Best Defense

Malcolm Muggeridge once called legal abortion "a slippery slope." Many agree, fearing that legal abortion is just the first step down a slippery slope that will eventually deliver us into a world in which individual lives are readily expendable "in the interests of society." The downward slide that is forecast sees abortion leading to infanticide and infanticide to "mercy killings," of every sort, not only to "weed out" the physical and mental "defectives," but also perhaps the "unproductive" elderly, those who are politically or socially "deviant," and any number of minorities which might be perceived, at any given time, as a threat to society. Several pro-abortion spokesmen have, in fact, endorsed infanticide under various circumstances, and some hospitals have made it a policy to "allow" some defective newborn babies to die by withdrawing food and medical care. Numerous "death-with-dignity" bills have been introduced into state legislatures, aimed at making it legal for doctors to put to death patients who request it or whose relatives request it.

But if we are on a slippery slope, there are some who have spoken and are speaking out, pointing to the dangers, trying to prevent further slippage. Dr. Jonathan H. Pincus of Yale has stated: "I have yet to hear of a set of guidelines for euthanasia ["mercy killing"] which would not lead to terrible abuses. . . ." Margaret Mead once said: "Society always is attempting to make the physician into a killer—to kill the defective child at birth, to leave the sleeping pills beside the

131

bed of the cancer patient. . . . It is the duty of society to protect the physician from such requests."[18]

Jean Rostand said:

> For my part, I believe there is no life so degraded, debased, deteriorated or impoverished that it does not deserve respect and is not worth defending with zeal and conviction. . . . Above all, I believe that a terrible precedent would be established if we agreed that a life could be allowed to end because it is not worth preserving since the notion of biological worthiness, even if carefully circumscribed at first, would soon become broader and less precise. After eliminating what was no longer human, the next step would be to eliminate what was not sufficiently human, and finally nothing would be spared except what fit a certain ideal concept of humanity.[19]

Dr. Viktor Frankl, the great Viennese psychotherapist, has stated:

> Even a man who finds himself in the greatest distress, in which neither activity nor creativity can bring values to his life, nor experience give meaning to it—even such a man can still give his life meaning by the way he faces his fate, his distress. By taking his unavoidable suffering upon himself he may yet realize values. Thus, life has meaning to the last breath.[20]

Archibald Cox, famous for his role as Watergate special prosecutor, clearly saw in the 1973 Supreme Court decision a peril of the slippery-slope variety. In his book, *The Role of the Supreme Court in American Government,* Cox wrote:

> The opinion fails even to consider what I would suppose to be the most compelling interest of the State in prohibiting abortion: the interest of maintaining that respect for the paramount sanctity of human life which has always been at the center of Western civilization.[21]

[18]Quoted in Maurice Levine, *Psychiatry and Ethics* (New York: George Braziller, 1972), 324-325.
[19]*Humanly Possible.*
[20]*Man's Search for Meaning* (Boston: Beacon Press, 1959).
[21](New York: Oxford Univ. Press, 1976).

The Supreme Court of West Germany, in limiting access to abortion in that country, was also obviously aware of a potentially slippery slope. "We cannot ignore the educational impact of abortion on the respect of life," it declared. But then, Germany had been down the slippery slope before—all the way down. Perhaps the justices of that court recalled the words of George Santayana: "Those who cannot remember the past are condemned to repeat it."

Finally, however, there is only one thing, barring divine intervention, that can preserve life—and that is life itself. An old saying claims that "familiarity breeds contempt." I dispute that. Studies have shown that people express a greater willingness to harm or kill another person if the victim is strange, alien, or unknown to them. Place the victim out of sight and require only that a button be pushed to effect the execution, and the task becomes easier still. But *see, know, understand* the other person—the intended victim—and it becomes difficult, for some impossible, to inflict death or serious injury upon that person. That is why, ultimately, the best argument against abortion is the unborn life itself, a life all of us should seek to see, know, and understand better.

9

The Human Element

Four Case Histories

There now exists a large network of organizations and "support groups" to assist women who want to have abortions. Planned Parenthood and other organizations have formidable funding with which to spread the word that abortions are readily available. The message goes out that abortions are "all right" morally, physically, and psychologically. I have heard colleagues tell women that having an abortion is no worse than "having a cold." I have even heard women told that "abortions are safer than pregnancy."

What gets lost in the propaganda barrage is the fact that not *all* abortions are safe and not *all* women are happy they had them. Many women undoubtedly have "uneventful" abortions, without either serious physical or psychological complications. But as some of the studies cited earlier in this book prove, complications *do* occur and far more often than many of the pro-abortionists want to admit. Again, there is very often a subtle withholding of information—a withholding that sometimes proceeds at an unconscious level, a withholding that denies the woman who is thinking of having an abortion the opportunity to make a fully informed decision.

In particular, the possible psychological complications of

abortion are given short shrift. Instead, emphasis is placed on the psychological burdens suffered by those women who are *denied* abortion. I am not going to fall into the trap of suggesting, as a few anti-abortionists have, that *most* abortions lead to severe remorse, depression, even suicide. Such claims are easily and properly discredited. But it is past time that equally outrageous claims to the contrary—that *most* abortions are casual matters soon forgotten—be laid to rest. It is also time to dispel the myth that women who are denied abortions or who are persuaded not to have them inevitably end up miserable, abusive of their "unwanted" offspring, or worse.

I do not claim that the case histories that follow are "typical" of all who must make a personal decision on abortion. But each case serves in a different way to demonstrate some of the complex psychological processes and surprises that arise in the course of the abortion drama. Names and various details have been changed to protect the identities of those involved.

Jennifer

Jennifer, age twenty, was already thirteen weeks pregnant when she came to me. I knew her family and had seen her off and on over the years. I knew that she was unmarried and in college. When I confirmed the pregnancy, she burst into tears, saying, "I have to get rid of it." I asked her why she had waited so long. She said that she thought she could be pregnant but had desperately been hoping that wasn't the case.

"I hoped it would be a tumor, anything but a baby," she said wryly.

I couldn't help grimacing a little at that statement. I had heard that sort of sentiment too often before. I have never been able to understand how we as a society can regard a baby, on the one hand, as something to prize above almost everything else, and then, on the other hand, under other circumstances, as something almost worse than a cancer.

136

In any event, for all her intelligence and sophistication, Jennifer had put off facing the inevitable. Abortion at this point would entail far greater risk than one performed weeks earlier. She could tell I was still wondering *why?*

The answer had to do with the young man who was the apparent father of this unwanted life-in-the-womb. Jennifer declared that she was in love with him, that he was "different" from all the other young men in her life and that she had "messed up" with her birth control and accidentally become pregnant. Whatever chance she had with Bob, the young man, would, she said, be "ruined" if he found out that she had "carelessly jeopardized both of our careers" by becoming pregnant. She said that she was not "entirely" certain that Bob loved her as much as she loved him. But he was "so decent," she added, that if she told him she was pregnant with his child he would marry her "in a minute—and then resent me for the rest of his life."

I told Jennifer that I had great confidence in her as a judge of character. I knew she was not the type to fall head over heels in love with the first man to smile at her. She was bright and generally very insightful. I told her that if Bob was all that he seemed to be, she should trust her own judgment of him and tell him the truth. I said I felt he would react truthfully in return or that, in any event, Jennifer would be able to gauge his true feelings.

I also argued that it takes two to make a baby and that it should take two to *unmake* one. It's unfair, I said, to leave the father out of the picture.

But Jennifer was having none of it. She'd thought about "all those things," she said, and she just couldn't risk telling Bob. "It would kill me," she insisted, "if this ruined things for us."

She asked me to perform the abortion. I told her I would not. She acted as if I had slapped her in the face, taking my refusal personally. I explained, however, that I do not perform abortions, having long since come to the conclusion that the unborn constitutes human life worthy of protection. Jennifer was clearly in no mood for a lecture on that score, however, and I was not about to offer one unbidden. I told her that I sympathized with her and suggested she think more about what she was contemplating before proceeding.

Two months later Jennifer returned to see me. I didn't have to look at her twice to conclude that she was more distraught this time than when I had last seen her. She'd had the abortion, she said, and she wanted me to examine her to make sure she had fully recovered. Actually, it soon became evident, she had come to talk, though at first she said little of anything.

"Well, I told him," she blurted suddenly. So that was it. I have to admit my heart sank a little: She had taken my advice and it had obviously backfired. That's what I thought until Jennifer added: "I told him *after* I'd done it." She said she had felt "sick and lousy and drained" both physically and psychologically in the days right after the abortion, and Bob kept questioning her about what was wrong.

"I guess I needed some support from him just then. My guard was down and I just told him. I don't know. Maybe I thought he'd think I loved him even more because I'd sacrificed the baby. Something dumb like that."

And?

"He didn't react at all like I thought he would. He went white. And he got angry. He tried to hide it for a while, but it all came out. It all blew up about a week after that."

What it came down to, Jennifer admitted, was this: "He felt robbed." Robbed of his right to participate in a life-and-death decision, robbed of the child that was partly his. As for the relationship, "He tried to pretend it was the same for a while, but it didn't work. It's over. I know that now."

Ellen

In some respects, Ellen is the "flip side" of Jennifer. She had been married for some years and had one child, a son, who was now in his teens. Now she found herself unexpectedly pregnant again—and she was delighted.

On a follow-up visit, however, her mood had changed. Jack, her husband, did not share her enthusiasm over the pregnancy and in fact had accused her of arranging for the "accident." She denied that she had done this, but made it clear to me again that she was happy to be pregnant and hoped the baby would be a girl. She had always wanted a daughter, she confided. Jack had wanted a son, and when their first child turned out to be a boy, he had not wanted more children.

On her third visit Ellen abruptly announced that she wanted an abortion. In view of what had gone before, I was considerably taken aback by this request.

Ellen explained that she had seen "Jack's point of view." Ellen was in her late thirties and Jack was forty-five. "We're too old to be new parents," Ellen said. In addition, Jack had made it clear that Ellen was a necessary fixture in his business life, that he needed her at his side, traveling with him and so on in the course of managing their business. Ellen spoke with some excitement of an extensive trip through Europe and Asia Jack was planning for them that summer. Obviously she couldn't make the trip, which would be quite strenuous, if she were pregnant—or so she said. Moreover, she reported, "Jack wants his wife slim and beautiful, not pregnant and beautiful." She laughed as she said this, but there was something about her merriment that struck me as hollow. It seemed to me there was more here than Ellen was admitting.

I told Ellen that, her age notwithstanding, there was certainly no medical indication for an abortion and that I wouldn't perform one in any event. I said I had no doubt that many other doctors would. The idea that all or even a significant proportion of abortions are performed for some medical reason has long since become a joke in the medical profession. Almost all abortions are purely elective, and everyone in the profession knows it, though a few still won't admit it.

And Ellen did, indeed, have her abortion, just a week after she saw me on that third occasion. I thought I might not see her again. If I didn't, it wouldn't be the first time that a patient had stopped consulting me after I refused to perform an abortion.

But about a year later, Ellen did return. The first thing she told me was that Jack was divorcing her. Then she let it all spill out—her overwhelming bitterness at having "done everything his way, including that abortion," only to have him leave her for another woman, a woman he'd been clandestinely having an affair with for some years. Now Ellen felt doubly used; Jack, she complained, had even "denied" her the baby she had so badly wanted so that she could continue to be his business "prop," as she put it.

Ellen was furious with Jack and even more furious with herself. She was also riddled with guilt over the abortion, which now seemed "a complete waste." Jack, she felt, "might at least have left me with the baby."

I saw Ellen several more times over the years. She did not remarry. Once she commented that she no longer felt "worthy" of motherhood. It can be argued, of course, that Ellen perhaps suffered from some serious neuroses to begin with. But it can hardly be argued that the abortion did other than worsen her condition considerably. My complaint in this case is that a doctor could so easily be found who was quite willing to perform an abortion without even the slightest medical indication for one. I am also deeply concerned when abortions are so casually carried out without careful evaluation of the possible psychological consequences.

Carrie

Carrie's was a dramatic story, almost the stuff movies are made of. She wasn't my patient, but I chatted with her once; I knew her doctor and I knew what had happened. Carrie came from what many would call "the best of families." Her parents were socially prominent people. Carrie had almost reached her seventeenth birthday when she became pregnant.

Precocious in every way, Carrie did not hesitate to tell her parents what had happened. She also told them who the boy involved was and announced that they wanted to keep the baby and intended to get married in a few years. Carrie's parents were horrified. Carrie's father forbade her to see the boy, also a minor, ever again. Carrie's parents did not even want the boy's parents, active in the same social circle, to know of the pregnancy.

Over Carrie's vigorous protestations, arrangements were

made for an abortion in a city two thousand miles from home. An aunt and uncle were to see to it that the abortion was carried out. The plan was then to send Carrie to a school in Europe. Her friends, including the boy who was the father of Carrie's child, were told that she had come down with a serious illness and had been sent to a treatment center abroad. The boy tried everything he could think of to find out where Carrie had gone, but he was unable to do so. At one point he and Carrie's father actually exchanged blows, and the boy was arrested.

Meanwhile, Carrie had been taken to the opposite coast. One day before her scheduled abortion she "escaped," as she later put it, and called her boyfriend, who promptly ran away from home and met Carrie at a prearranged location. Both sets of parents initiated searches to no avail. The first news they received that the young couple was all right came months later when both families received identical birth announcements. Carrie had had her baby. The young couple later married and are still together.

Too often, in my experience, girls and women have abortions not so much because *they* want them, but rather because they receive no support—moral, economic, or otherwise—for carrying their babies to term. Too often it is the parents of the unwed mother who press for the abortion. Or it is a husband or boyfriend who wants the woman to abort. Or the woman *thinks* the boyfriend wants her to have one, and so on.

Too often there is a woeful lack of reflection. The surprise of pregnancy is followed, as if inevitable, by the grim decision to have an abortion. I have found that "cooling-off" periods can have profound impact. What appears "necessary" today often appears foolhardy tomorrow.

Samantha

Samantha was pregnant for the fourth time. She had three healthy children, but when she learned she was pregnant this time she expressed concern because she was forty years old. Amniocentesis was performed during the seventeenth week of pregnancy to discover whether Samantha's baby was ge-

141

netically normal: Older women are at higher risk of giving birth to babies with various genetic anomalies.

As it turned out, there *was* something wrong. The tests showed that Samantha's baby, a boy, was suffering from Down's syndrome, or mongolism. If permitted to live, the child would suffer from mental retardation. Many parents upon receiving such news, immediately order an abortion. Samantha, however, surprised herself.

"I'd thought all along," she recalled, "that if something turned up like this, I would instantly opt for the abortion. I remember the doctors waiting for me to give them the go-ahead, to say I wanted the abortion. My husband was waiting too, I know, even though he didn't press the matter right away. But I just couldn't do it. I thought, well, maybe in a day or two I'll come to my senses and say, yes, let's have the abortion. But it didn't work that way. A few days later I felt even more certain I wanted to have that baby."

Samantha's decision nearly wrecked her marriage. Her husband finally let it be known that he thought she was crazy for refusing the abortion. Samantha's doctor at that time also did little to hide his feelings. Even Samantha's oldest child got into the act, announcing he didn't want "a retard" for a brother.

"I don't know how I withstood all of this," Samantha says. "I wasn't raised in a religion that thinks abortion is immoral, or anything like that. It was just something inside me that said, this is my baby and I can't abandon it now. I did a lot of study, and I got a lot of reinforcement and moral support from other families that have handicapped children. It struck me how much love there was in these families and how closely tied together they were. Finally even my husband decided to put a good face on it, though I could tell he was still scared to death. So was I, to tell the truth."

Several years have now passed since Samantha's "special" child was born. The boy's older brother is now fiercely protective of him. So is the boy's father. "This has pulled us together like nothing else ever could have," Samantha concludes. "We've learned the real meaning of being a family. We owe this child far more than we can ever repay."

10

Family Planning Versus Abortion

The "Wanted Child" Issue Revisited

I find it unfortunate that some people who oppose abortion shy away from family planning and the birth control that such planning encompasses. Some seem to fear that the mere acknowledgment that it is better to plan one's family than simply to "let it happen" gives aid and comfort to the pro-abortionists. Some of those who yield to this fear, I believe, are unwittingly letting themselves be manipulated by pro-abortion illogic. This is a tricky but very important business, so let's try to sort it out.

"Every child a *wanted* child" has become a slogan of Planned Parenthood and the pro-abortion lobby in this country. The idea is that if a child is unwanted, then it is not going to be loved and properly cared for; thus, the pro-abortionists argue, it is better off being denied further life. I have responded to this argument already: One's degree of "wantedness" should never be permitted to determine whether one lives or dies. And in any event, the state of being wanted is highly relative; those unwanted today may be very much wanted in the future.

We have to be careful not to throw the good out with   **143** the bad. In rejecting the "wantedness" argument, we mustn't go one step further and, in a mistaken effort to be "consistent," reject the whole concept of family planning as well. "Planning," in other words, must not become confused with this distorted notion of "wanting." The pro-abortionists are never more delighted than when the other side takes a hidebound position against all family planning; it is that sort of rigidity that permits those who favor abortion to tar those who don't as "moral neanderthals" who would not only deny women the "right" to abort, but also the right *not* to become pregnant in the first place.

Perspective is the key. It *is* clearly better to plan one's family; it certainly is better to want the child in the womb than not to want it. But this does not mean that if a child is conceived which you did not plan for and perhaps do not even want at this point, you are in any way justified in killing it. There is absolutely nothing illogical or inconsistent about supporting family planning *and* opposing abortion. To do otherwise is illogical.

We owe it to ourselves and our prospective children to assume procreative responsibility. Helping to bring a new life into the world is not something we should take lightly. We should see to it that we are up to the task—emotionally, physically, mentally, spiritually, even economically. Pregnancies that "just happen" are more likely than those that are planned to put both mother and baby in jeopardy. They may also endanger marriages. If, through our own failure to assume responsibility, we place ourselves or our unborn children in danger, then we can scarcely be said to show respect for life. It should be recognized that there is more than one form of abortion. Some spontaneous abortions (miscarriages) are unavoidable; others are not. Many could be prevented through prudent family planning.

The crux of family planning is deciding when it is best to have children. Then we have to devise means of having children at that time—and not at some other time. So there are two challenges inherent in family planning: getting pregnant and not getting pregnant. That may seem simple and obvious enough, but in fact, it often isn't so simple. Some do all the appropriate planning only to discover they can't conceive when they want to, for one reason or another. Others know they don't want to conceive at particular times and then must figure out how best to avoid conception. For all the progress medical science has made, we still have not achieved anything approaching an ideal contraceptive. Those who oppose abortion, moreover, face special problems, for they may have heard that some commonly used forms of "contraception" are actually abortifacients—that is, that they "work," not by preventing conception, but rather, by aborting the very early embryo or zygote.

Before we turn to a discussion of fertility control, let's examine a number of things I ask couples to consider before setting out to create new life.

Are You Ready to Have a Baby? (A Checklist)

• *Why do we want a baby?* This is the first question you and your mate should ask yourselves, once you've begun thinking about having a child. If only one of you thinks having a baby is a good idea, you are flirting with danger. I have seen many a marriage go astray because one partner was considerably less sure about this than the other. Real danger emerges when a woman unilaterally decides to get pregnant and neglects to consult her husband. The woman may covertly stop using birth control and then suddenly announce to her husband, as one of my patients did, "Guess what, darling, *we're* pregnant!" The motivation behind this kind of surprise may be desperation. Sometimes women think that a marriage that's beginning to go sour can be sweetened and saved by pregnancy. In my experience with thousands of couples, the opposite is usually true. The strains of an unplanned pregnancy will shatter a shaky marriage if anything will. And in any event, having a baby to try to save a tottering marriage is terribly unfair to the baby.

Of course, it is sometimes the husband who pushes for the pregnancy against his wife's will. More than one husband, in the privacy of the doctor's office, has admitted to covertly puncturing condoms in order to impregnate wives who did not want another child. In such instances the husbands have simply claimed, "There must have been an accident." On being questioned, such men often admit that they were worried that their wives were about to leave them; in effect they sought to "tie down" their wives by getting them pregnant. Other men have been motivated by the desire to "escape" from their wives by keeping them pregnant, with the explanation that "while she's pregnant, she's preoccupied and doesn't bother me." Such ploys at best merely delay the day of marital reckoning.

I have seen many unwed girls (and even many adult women) who have purposely become pregnant in order to "force" a boyfriend to enter into marriage. I've also seen many young married couples who have had babies before they really wanted them, simply because they thought it the "adult" thing to do or because relatives and friends pressured them to have children. Then there are the couples who decide to have children in pursuit of some unfulfilled fantasy; these unhappy individuals impose *their* dreams on their children, trying to make a son, for example, into a great baseball player or a daughter into a world-famous ballerina. All such motivations mean trouble—usually lots of it.

Communication is the key. Both partners must want to have a baby. It is perfectly fine—even essential—to feel that having a child will deepen the bonds of marriage and intensify the love relationship, provided the relationship is in good shape to begin with. If it is not, then it should be put in order before any effort is made to have a baby. Counting on the child to patch things up is unreasonable and irresponsible. It is also perfectly fine—even healthy—to want to see something of yourselves perpetuated in your offspring, provided you don't go over board and expect virtual "chips off the old block."

It is wise for the marital partners to discuss their ideas about raising children in detail before they have any. Probably you will find common ground; yet, occasionally such discussions will reveal serious and irreconcilable differences concerning child-rearing. If these arise, you may want to think again before proceeding. Ideally, of course, such matters will have been discussed *before* marriage. In any event, if you cannot agree that the best reason for having babies is that you want and love children, you should reconsider the matter.

• *Are we emotionally and financially suited for parenthood at this time?* If you are able to rationally and calmly discuss the pros and cons of having a baby with your mate, the chances are your overall emotional stability is good. You should give special thought, however, to how well you relate to children. Some people admit that they don't particularly like *other* people's children, but then blithely assume that "it will be different when I have my own." Don't count on it. If other people's children constantly get on your nerves, it is sheer arrogance and foolhardiness to imagine that your own children will be so "perfect" that you'll have no difficulty in adapting to parenthood.

Here again, communication is all-important. Many couples assume that if the woman feels all right about having a baby, everything will be fine. Men are generally more guarded in their emotions than are women. I have found it not at all uncommon for women, especially those carrying their first babies, to suddenly discover "another side" to their husbands. Often these women complain that their husbands are "less mature" than previously imagined. The husband may discover this about himself, as well, for pregnancy imposes certain strains on the unprepared, just as it confers many joys on those who are well-prepared.

During the pregnancy, a man may begin to see his wife in a different light and may have some difficulty coping with what he sees. Some men find it difficult to reconcile the image of their wives as lovers with the emerging image of them as mothers. Then, too, pregnancy may interrupt a couple's sexual relationship, for either physical or psychological reasons. Some men find themselves jealous, not only of the unborn for taking up so much of their wives' time, but also sometimes of their wives themselves. All of this makes it evident that the man's needs should be given equal consideration with the woman's in planning a pregnancy.

147

Our emotional state is often determined, in part, by our financial state. Oddly, this is something many couples are reluctant to admit. In my experience, those couples who do admit it and plan accordingly usually have happier, more successful pregnancies. The feeling that "money shouldn't matter" is a mistaken one, in my view. When couples are barely making ends meet financially, a new pregnancy can put dangerous strains on an otherwise good relationship. I recall one couple who decided to "just go ahead and have a baby" even though they admitted they couldn't afford another child. They thought it was the noble thing to do, or at least the romantic thing; the money would take care of itself. It didn't. In fact, there were costly complications during the pregnancy that strained the couple's finances to the limit and threatened to shatter their marriage. The husband was particularly bitter about the financial burden, and the wife responded by abruptly deciding (without consulting anyone) to have an abortion.

• *Are we physically ready?* Pregnancy is an important physical event. Both husband and wife should be "in shape" for it. It is a good idea for both partners to have a physical checkup early on in planning a child. The doctor giving the examinations should be told of the plans to have a baby. If there is any history of genetic abnormality on either side of the family, this should be discussed with the doctor. If you think there is a potential for passing some problem on to your prospective children, there are various genetic screening tests the doctor can tell you about. Be aware that some genetic problems can be passed on and manifest themselves in the next generation even if they are not evident in you.

Your physical readiness will be determined in part by the date of any previous pregnancy. One of the most important aspects of family planning is the *spacing of your children.* Many babies are lost because one pregnancy follows another too closely. Most doctors will tell you that a year between pregnancies should be the bare minimum. My experience has convinced me that *eighteen months* should be considered the minimum if you really want to be safe. We could reduce fetal deaths and newborn deaths very dramatically if we would wait at least eighteen months between pregnancies. There is no virtue in having one baby right after another, exposing innocent lives to prematurity, low birth weights, and other causes of perinatal death and disability.

The doctor you consult before you become pregnant will help you assess the advisability of pregnancy in terms of your age as well as your general health. The doctor who is doing his job will tell you that pregnancy in the late thirties or older carries noticeably higher risk than pregnancy in the twenties and early thirties. There is a significantly higher incidence of prematurity and miscarriage among teen-age mothers than there is among women in the optimal pregnancy range (twenty to thirty-five). This is because the teenager's body is still maturing and is not yet as fully equipped for pregnancy as it will be in a few years. Pregnancy after age thirty-five is also considered riskier; women older than thirty-five, however, often have completely normal pregnancies. Much depends upon the individual and her health. That is why an examination is important.

● *Okay, we're ready. How long should we wait to try after going off birth control?* If you have been using the Pill, you should not attempt to become pregnant until you have been off oral contraceptives for *at least three months.* Women who conceive too soon after going off the Pill have a measurably increased chance of having babies with various birth defects. You must let your body return to normal after discontinuing the Pill. Women under my care are told to wait until they have had at least two consecutive menstrual cycles with normal bleeding, before trying to get pregnant. Depending in part on how long you have been using the Pill and in part on your own biochemistry, you may have to wait several months before you experience two normal cycles in a row. *But do wait.* And in the meantime use some alternative method of birth control, such as condoms and/or diaphragm and spermicidal jelly, foam, or cream.

If you have been using an IUD (intrauterine device), you will obviously want to have it removed before attempting   **149** pregnancy. Occasionally pregnancies occur while IUDs are in place, often leading to spontaneous abortion. If a pregnancy does occur with an IUD in place, the device should be removed as quickly as possible.

Birth Control

Although there are a significant number of people who suffer from one form of infertility or another at some point in their lives, the challenge for most lies not in achieving pregnancy, but in *avoiding* it. The various forms of birth control can seem a confusing puzzle at times, not only because there is such a variety of choices, but also because there is so much conflicting information. People who are concerned about abortion are often troubled by doubts about the mode of action of the various methods. Which methods truly prevent conception from occurring? Which act as abortifacients by killing the zygote or preventing it from implanting in the womb? Let's examine each of the major forms of birth control, in regard to both their relative effectiveness and their modes of action.

• *The Pill.* What most people call "the Pill" is actually a large family of oral contraceptives. There are more than two dozen pills on the market today, all consisting of various synthetic combinations of the hormones estrogen and progesterone or, in a few cases, progesterone alone. How is it that these two hormones can be used to prevent pregnancy when in fact they are *essential* for pregnancy? The ovaries produce these hormones in a carefully programmed fashion to ensure that an egg will mature and emerge from the ovary at just the right time and that the lining of the uterus will be receptive at just the right time. The estrogen acts primarily on the egg, and the progesterone primarily on the lining of the womb, getting it ready for the egg.

When we add synthetic versions of these hormones into the system via the Pill, the body's monitoring apparatus in the brain is tricked into halting the body's own production of these substances. The monitors "notice" that there is al-

150

ready enough of these hormones in the system, so they signal the ovaries to stop producing them. The ovaries "shut down," and ovulation ceases. The synthetic hormones, however, are still capable of building up the lining of the womb; thus, when the Pill is briefly withdrawn, the lining breaks down and menstrual bleeding ensues. The Pill is popular with some women because it tends in this way to "regularize" their menstrual cycles.

To the extent that the Pill acts to prevent ovulation, it is a true contraceptive. The progesterone-only preparations, however, are more likely to be abortifacient, allowing ovulation but preventing implantation. And the Pill in any form appears likely to allow ovulation from time to time in some women. On such occasions, fertilization may occur despite the Pill. It is unlikely, however, that the fertilized egg will implant; even if it does, the process will be interrupted in most cases by continued use of the Pill. The Pill therefore has to be considered at least potentially abortifacient in its mode of action.

The effectiveness of the Pill is unquestioned. Nothing can equal it as a method of birth control except complete abstinence. Yet it is not the ideal form of birth control many believed it to be in the late 1950s and early 1960s. After the euphoria of its introduction wore off, women and their doctors began worrying—for good reason—about its many complications and side effects, which include nausea and vomiting, breast tenderness, the aggravation of some skin problems and migraine headaches, blood-clotting problems, and fatal heart attacks.

I believe that it is potentially dangerous for adolescent girls to use the Pill, because it can interfere with many hormonal/metabolic processes that should not be disturbed at that age in particular. Unfortunately, the Pill remains the most popular form of birth control among adolescents. It is also contraindicated for women with diabetes, high blood pressure, and various other disorders. I suggest that each woman who is thinking of using the Pill first consult her physician to explore particular risks. I also suggest that she ask about nutritional supplementation to the Pill. This is important, because the use of oral contraceptives can deplete levels of various nutrients. I advise supplementation with folic acid and the vitamin B complex, but you should consult your doctor.

For some time there were fears that the Pill might cause cancer or aggravate existing cancers. Long-range studies have now largely discounted that possibility. In fact, these same studies have indicated that the Pill can actually help prevent cancers of certain types, principally ovarian cancer and cancer of the endometrium (uterine wall). Early indications that the Pill might promote breast cancers have not been confirmed in extensive follow-up studies.

Offsetting this good news, however, is equally strong evidence—from the same studies—that using the Pill significantly increases a woman's chance of having a fatal heart attack. A user of the Pill is three times more likely to have a fatal heart attack than a non-user. The risk goes up with age, and the highest risk is for women who take the Pill and also smoke. These studies indicate that users of the Pill are at significantly higher risk of dying from blood clots that break loose in the blood stream and lodge in the lungs.

I do not recommend use of the Pill for women who smoke, who are over thirty-five, who have high blood pressure, who have varicose veins, who have evidence of blood clotting or a known predisposition thereto, or who have sexual intercourse infrequently. For all these women, the risks of the Pill far outweigh the benefits. Moreover, if the possible abortifacient activity of the Pill concerns you, then obviously you should seek another form of birth control even if you do not fit into any of the foregoing categories. Many other methods are almost as effective as the Pill and have far fewer dangerous side effects.

• *Intrauterine Devices (IUDs).* IUDs are small objects of varying shapes, made of plastic or sometimes metal, which are inserted in the womb and left there. They are highly effective—but not as contraceptives. They are almost always abortifacient in their mode of action. As foreign bodies in the uterus, they create an environment that is hostile to the fertilized ovum. The IUD irritates the lining of the womb and causes the cells of that lining to produce substances that either destroy the zygote when it arrives or prevent it from implanting. The reactive mechanisms that the IUD excite may also interfere with the processes by which the egg is transported down the fallopian tube.

Toleration of IUDs varies widely from woman to woman. They are not recommended under any circumstances for women who have never been pregnant. This is because the relatively small size of the uterus and the narrowness of the cervical canal in such women make them unsuitable. The IUDs do not influence the woman's hormonal cycles, but they are not free from complications. Mild side effects may include heavier than normal menstrual bleeding, cramping and other discomfort. Serious side effects may include life-threatening infections, very heavy bleeding, and perforation of the uterus. They should not be used in women who suffer from highly painful menstruation, history of heavy bleeding, anatomical anomalies of the uterus and other reproductive organs, or uterine infections.

Because of their clear-cut abortifacient action, I cannot recommend IUDs under any circumstances.

• *Diaphragm.* The diaphragm is perhaps the most important of the "barrier" methods of birth control. It is a rubber cap that fits over the cervix. A collapsible metal spring, embedded in the rim of the cap, helps hold it in place. The diaphragm must initially be fitted by a physician to make sure that it fits snugly over the cervix. Thereafter the woman can easily remove and reinsert it whenever she desires. Used properly, the diaphragm is very effective; it prevents conception by keeping the sperm from passing through the cervix and into the uterus. Some six million American women now use barrier methods of birth control, a number that has been growing steadily at the same time that use of the Pill has been declining.

The diaphragm's effectiveness is further enhanced by the addition of spermicidal jelly, cream, or foam, which is applied to the rim and inside the diaphragm. I recommend that the diaphragm always be used in conjunction with a spermicidal substance. Under such circumstances its effectiveness can approach that of the Pill. It should be checked by a physician every two years, however, and it must be refitted at the end of each pregnancy to accommodate the changed shape and size of the cervix. The diaphragm and spermicidal substance should be inserted before intercourse and then left in place for at least six hours afterward. It may be left in place for up to twenty-four hours, after which it should be removed, cleaned, and stored for future use.

Diaphragms (and some other barrier methods) have a very beneficial side effect. Recent research has shown that women who use diaphragms are 40 percent less likely than other women to develop pelvic inflammatory disease, a sexually transmitted infection that is a leading cause of dangerous ectopic pregnancies and infertility. This disease currently afflicts more than one million American women each year at a cost of more than $3 billion nationwide. The disease can be very painful and may require hospitalization and surgery in some instances. Condoms and spermicidal substances also confer some protection, but diaphragms provide the most.

• *Contraceptive Sponge.* I learned late in 1982 that an advisory committee of the federal Food and Drug Administration recommended immediate approval of a forty-eight-hour contraceptive sponge—a new type of barrier birth control—that may be available without prescription as you read this. It is already on the market in England. The sponge is said to be as effective as the diaphragm. The two-inch-long plastic sponge is presoaked in a spermicidal solution and has several potential advantages over the diaphragm. The sponge does not require a prescription and is projected to sell at a lower price. It doesn't need to be fitted by a doctor; it is simply inserted into the vagina by the woman and can be left in place for up to forty-eight hours without requiring any additional spermicide. Thereafter it is withdrawn and discarded. Fears that the sponge might promote toxic shock syndrome have not been borne out in extensive testing. This is, in my view, potentially one of the most important new developments in birth control. Since it is new, however, I suggest that you consult your doctor as to the status of the sponge prior to using it.

• *Cervical Cap.* This is a cuplike device that fits over the cervix. It is another barrier method and is similar to the diaphragm except that it is held in place by suction. It must be fitted by a physician, but unlike the diaphragm, it can be left in place for extended periods of time. Its effectiveness is increased, however, when it is removed prior to intercourse, treated with spermicidal substances, and then reinserted.

• *Condom.* This is a barrier method used by the male. It is a rubber sheath that is placed over the penis prior to intercourse. It retains the ejaculate and thus prevents conception. Condoms can be very effective; they seldom break. They do occasionally slip off, however, when the penis is withdrawn from the vagina at the end of intercourse. This is more likely to occur when withdrawal occurs after loss of erection. Slippage can easily be avoided by simply holding the condom firmly at the base of the penis during withdrawal. Some couples object to condoms on aesthetic grounds; others find them entirely satisfactory. Besides contraceptions, they offer the benefits of reducing the risks of contracting or passing on various forms of venereal disease. Even when used alone, they can be very effective if care is exercised during withdrawal. Used in conjunction with diaphragms and/or spermicidal substances, they are highly effective.

• *Spermicidal Foams, Jellies, Creams.* These substances all constitute barrier forms of birth control, acting to stop the sperm on the way to the egg. These are considerably less effective than the other barrier methods. Of these, the foams tend to be the most effective; the jellies and creams rank next in effectiveness; the tablets and suppositories are the least effective. There are numerous different products on the market; care must be taken to follow instructions with respect to application and timing. I recommend that spermicides be used only in conjunction with one of the other barrier methods.

155

• *Ovulation Method.* This is a "natural" method of birth control and one that is gaining in popularity. I have been teaching the method for years. It is based on learning how to determine the time of ovulation and subsequently avoiding unprotected intercourse during the fertile period. Some couples who use this method avoid intercourse entirely during the woman's fertile period; others use condoms and/or diaphragms during the fertile period and nothing during the nonfertile time. The ovulation method should not be confused with the so-called calendar rhythm method of natural birth control, which is far less effective. The ovulation method utilizes such factors as temperature charting and careful observation of cervical mucus, which has different characteristics at different stages of the monthly cycle. With proper training, I have found, women can use this method with a high degree of effectiveness.

Training, however, is the key. It would be irresponsible to try to teach the proper use of the method in the limited space available here. Some supervised instruction is recommended. Those interested should check their libraries for information on the subject: Look, for example, at the *Atlas of the Ovulation Method.*[1] Information on the availability of classes that teach the method in your area may be obtained by writing to the Couple to Couple League, 3621 Glenmore Avenue, P.O. Box 11084, Cincinnati, Ohio 45211.

An international scientific trial of the ovulation method was recently carried out in five socioeconomically divergent places. The method was taught as described in the *Atlas.* Most of the women involved were able to learn the method rapidly—a highly encouraging finding, since some critics of the method have claimed it is suitable only for the more sophisticated and literate. Results varied, but interestingly, they were *best* in the least-developed countries in which it was tested. *Research in Reproduction,* published by the International Planned Parenthood Federation in London, reported: "It is important

[1] E. L. Billings, J. J. Billings, and M. Cataranich (Melbourne, Australia, 1974).

to note that the method was relatively successful in all five of the countries, of which three were developing nations."[2]

- *Calendar Rhythm.* This method involves keeping records of each menstrual cycle for a period of eight to twelve months. It depends upon women being able to figure out their "average" cycles on the basis of calendar calculations. Calendar rhythm is a "numbers game"—and one you are likely to lose. I do not recommend its use because of its low effectiveness. If your religion dictates that no "unnatural" method of birth control be used, then you should lose no time learning the ovulation method of birth control, which is far more effective.

- *Douching.* This is another method I try to discourage. The idea here is to have unrestricted intercourse (i.e., without birth control) and then, immediately afterward, douche with a sperm-killing solution. This is a bad idea because sperm may get through the cervix before you douche, no matter how fast you are. And in any event, who wants to have to dash for the bathroom the very second intercourse is over? This is a highly unreliable method.

- *Coitus Interruptus.* This age-old method, which involves interruption of intercourse by withdrawal of the penis *before* ejaculation, is more effective than douching, but it is not very satisfying for either marital partner. Furthermore, it is far from failsafe, because some sperm often emerge before ejaculation. This is not a reliable method.

- *Vasectomy (Male Sterilization).* This relatively simple surgical procedure may be performed in a doctor's office under local anesthesia. It rarely requires more than fifteen to thirty minutes. Small incisions are made on each side of the scrotum, allowing access to the sperm ducts, which are then tied and cut. This prevents the sperm from escaping during ejaculation. Ejaculation of seminal fluid without sperm still

[2]Vol. 14, no. 3 (July 1982):11.

occurs, and vasectomy does not affect a man's sex drive. I have not been enthusiastic about vasectomies, because most of them are irreversible; if a man has one and then decides later that he wants children, he may not be able to have them. In addition, some evidence has come to light in recent years that vasectomized men may be more susceptible than average to autoimmune diseases and certain cardiovascular problems. The possible reasons for this remain complex and not entirely clear. You should discuss the pros and cons with your doctor if you are considering a vasectomy.

● *Tubal Ligation (Female Sterilization)*. This is commonly referred to as the "tube-tying" operation. It used to entail major surgery. Increasingly, however, doctors are using laparascopic procedures for the task. A small, pencil-like viewing device—the laparascope—can be inserted through a small abdominal incision for direct viewing of the fallopian tubes. Small instruments can be placed through another tiny incision to clip and tie the tubes, making it impossible for eggs to pass from the ovaries to the womb. The operation takes only about a half-hour and may require only one night in the hospital. As with vasectomy, there is no guarantee of reversibility. But unlike vasectomy, tubal ligation does not carry with it the risk of autoimmune and cardiovascular complications.

● *Experimental Methods.* "Morning-after," "month-after" and "once-a-month" pills, all in various experimental stages of development, are abortifacients. They destroy the zygote or prevent or disrupt implantation. Long-acting injectable substances designed to prevent ovulation would, on the face of it, be contraceptive in mode of action, but some of the ambiguities that relate to the Pill are liable to relate as well to these substances. The government's Office of Technology Assessment released a study in 1982 predicting that significantly improved condoms will probably be available before 1990. Also predicted for arrival within the next decade are disposable "one-size-fits-all" diaphragms and improved techniques for timing ovulation, making natural birth control easier to use and more reliable over a longer period of time. Sperm-suppressing drugs may also be on the market within a decade, according to this study, which predicts that before the end of the century, birth-control vaccines may also be widely available.

If Family Planning Fails: Alternatives to Abortion

Even the best plans sometimes fail. If a pregnancy occurs despite precautions, the issue of abortion almost inevitably arises. Even some people who recognize that abortion is the taking of meaningful human life may, when faced with an unwanted pregnancy, seriously consider something they would otherwise abhor. If a decision is finally made that another baby is definitely not wanted, I urge that the baby be spared. The chances are excellent that it can be adopted immediately after birth. The waiting list of couples who want to adopt babies is long and growing longer all the time.

There are numerous organizations that will help women through troubled pregnancies. Perhaps the most prominent of these is Birthright, which was founded in Toronto, Canada, in 1968. Birthright has now spread throughout Canada, the United States, England, and some other parts of the world. Birthright gives prospective mothers both psychological and financial help. There are more than a thousand Birthright centers in the United States alone. You may obtain information on centers in your area by writing to Birthright, 699 Coxwell Avenue, Toronto, Ontario, Canada.

Most Birthright centers are nonsectarian; a few are sponsored by various church groups. They all respect one's right to privacy. Their services are entirely confidential. They leave the decision on whether to keep the baby or give it up for adoption to the mother. They will help arrange for adoption if that is the choice.

Other organizations offer help as well. Information on a variety of such groups can be obtained from Alternatives to Abortion, Suite 511, Hillcrest Hotel, Toledo, Ohio.

Afterword

Abortion in the Future

Although the momentum is still very much with the pro-abortion forces, there are a number of factors at work that may diminish that momentum in the near future. Knowledge is one of them. Increasing familiarity with the unborn will breed respect, not contempt. The more we learn about life in the womb, the more difficult in conscience it will become for us to extinguish that life. Embryologists, fetologists, and neonatalists are extending the frontiers of our knowledge of this particular "inner space" every day. The fetus that was a "non-viable" nonentity just a few years ago is considered an entirely salvageable "premature baby" today.

Constantly improving birth control is another factor that will work against abortion. Within the next ten years it seems highly likely that new modes of fertility control will emerge that will make present methods look antiquated. With the advent of truly safe, entirely effective, and simple-to-use birth control, the "need" for abortion should diminish dramatically. Eventually it may take more effort to *become* pregnant than it will to *avoid* pregnancy.

Then too, the "cost-effectiveness" of abortion, as a solution to serious social problems, is likely to be successfully challenged in years to come. New data are emerging all the time that attest to the long-term costs and other negative sequellae of abortion. Pressure will mount to find other, better, safer, and more humane solutions.

I may be wrong, but I will predict that the "abortion era" will ultimately be judged by society with abhorrence. I have no doubt that the clamor for even more liberal abortion laws—ultimately making infanticide legal under a number of circumstances—will continue for some time. But few movements last forever, and as this one becomes increasingly callous and abusive of human rights, the tide of public opinion will begin to flow the other way. The extreme dangers and injustices of the "quality of life" ethic will finally be widely perceived as an ever-increasing number of social subgroups find themselves imperiled by that ethic. Then approval will yield to opprobrium.

Other factors may have an impact on abortion in the near term. After "test-tube babies"—produced in a procedure that involves implanting a woman's own egg back into the womb after fertilizing it in a laboratory container—will come embryo *transplants*. The woman who cannot produce eggs at all will still be able to become pregnant by having another woman's fertilized egg transplanted into her womb.

I am currently researching the possibility of salvaging embryos in very early abortions. I have demonstrated that it is possible to retrieve an intact embryo from the "products" of early suction curettage. It may prove feasible to transplant these aborted embryos to a recipient, allowing for a genuine program of "prenatal adoption."

The day may come when abortions will be few enough in number—reduced by public opinion, sex education, and vastly improved birth control—that all that do occur can end in life rather than death, either through transplantation or "ectogenesis," maintenance in life-support systems or "artificial wombs." Then "abortion" will assume a new—and more benign—definition.